THE PIMM PRINCIPLE

I = The

M = M.
w
n

M —

(P)   (I)   (M)   (M)
P   ↑   ↗   ↖
People Idea Model Market

$\pi = R - C$

7 — (P) --- (I) --- (M) --- (M)

Alignment
is clarity of
same purpose   is there   a connection

Alignment of P
idea models and mark
is the key to
foundational star

?
←

↑ Better

(P)   (M)   (I)

| VS. | ←

↓ worse
th.
(I)   (M)   (P)

☑

★ CAREFUL OF THIS TRAP!   (X)

CREES
even a theoretical model to make money.

Advance praise for
Heart, Smarts, Guts, and Luck

"This book provides the self-awareness and tools a leader needs at every stage of their business—from founding to scaling and beyond."
—Beth Comstock, Senior Vice President and Chief Marketing Officer, GE

"It's a rare treat to be able to learn directly from leaders who are so extraordinarily accomplished across multiple parts of the business world. *Hearts, Smarts, Guts, and Luck* is easy to relate to and relevant for any new or experienced entrepreneur."
—Joe Lonsdale, Cofounder, Palantir Technologies and Addepar, Inc.; Partner, Formation 8

"Finally, a book that investors like us can use with portfolio companies to engage them on their opportunity and challenges in growing businesses. Highly recommended."
—Yibing Wu, President, CITIC Private Equity

"A book by authors who care and know about the business-building journey because of their firsthand experiences and analytical acumen."
—Ram Charan, business consultant; coauthor, *The Talent Masters*

"Wisdom—some of it shockingly counterintuitive—from la crème de la crème of successful people from all walks of business and life, told not only in parables but with data and directness. The E.A.T. survey tells a timeless truth: that knowing oneself is fundamental to thriving."
—Patrick S. Chung, Partner, NEA

"An entertaining and informative 'wisdom collector' that sheds light on the many paths to entrepreneurial success. Every entrepreneur can benefit from studying what others have learned from the 'thrill of victory and the agony of defeat.'"
—William Sahlman, Professor of Business Administration, Harvard Business School

"Profoundly insightful. Transparent, gritty business advice from the entrepreneurs themselves and their inside stories. The Entrepreneurial Aptitude Test will change the way you understand yourself, your strengths, and how you work forever."
—David Kidder, Cofounder and CEO, Clickable

"*HSGL* is a book full of lessons that every entrepreneur should absorb and apply . . . you will learn the science, the art, and the stories to help create a successful business—and life."
—Jeff Rosenthal, Cofounder, Summit Series

"Tjan, Harrington, and Hsieh have nailed it. Building great companies takes a powerful cocktail of heart, smarts, guts, and luck. *HSGL* is filled to the brim with the lessons of innumerable successful entrepreneurs and the traits that helped them deliver on that success. Would-be entrepreneurs should give *HSGL* a careful read and measure themselves on the heart, smarts, guts, and luck scale."
—David Hornik, General Partner, August Capital

"Invaluable advice and timeless wisdom, written with clarity and practicality for any business leader."
—Dominic Barton, Global Managing Director, McKinsey & Company

HEART, Smarts, GUTS, and LUCK

WHAT IT TAKES TO BE AN ENTREPRENEUR AND BUILD A GREAT BUSINESS

ANTHONY K. TJAN, RICHARD J. HARRINGTON, TSUN-YAN HSIEH

Harvard Business Review Press

Boston, Massachusetts

Printed in the United States of America
10 9

Library of Congress Cataloging-in-Publication Data

Tjan, Anthony K.
    Heart, smarts, guts, and luck : what it takes to be an entrepreneur and build a great
business / Anthony K. Tjan, Richard J. Harrington, and Hsieh, Tsun-yan.
        p. cm.
    ISBN 978-1-4221-6194-4 (alk. paper)
    1. Entrepreneurship.   2. New business enterprises.   3. Success in business.
I. Harrington, Richard J.   II. Hsieh, Tsun-yan.   III. Title.
    HB615.T535 2012
    658.1'1—dc23

                                                                    2012003199

The paper used in this publication meets the requirements of the American National Standard for Permanence of Paper for Publications and Documents in Libraries and Archives
Z39.48-1992.

For our

Mamas and papas
Mentors and colleagues
Families and friends

Contents

OUR *Purpose* and a GUIDE to This BOOK

What does it take to be a great entrepreneur or business-builder? How do you find such a person? How do you become one?

These were some of the questions the three of us—more on who we are in a minute—asked ourselves when we embarked on the journey of writing this book. Along the way we asked a few more questions: What are the crucial character traits and habits for business-building success? Are they always the same, or do they depend on the circumstances? What are the things a business leader can learn versus the things that are innate? What role is played by luck, and can it be influenced? Do business *founders* possess fundamentally different strengths than the *scalers* who take businesses to the next level of growth? What are the most important crossroads that business-builders must face? Are there tools or experiences to help them with those decisions? Where can we look outside of the business world for clues and advice? And given how many business books and experts there are out there, what are the most useful lessons that *we* might impart?

What we've ended up with is a book that aims to leave readers with two things. The first is an increased *self-awareness* as it relates to starting and sustaining a business and the decisions we make on those issues. The second is the *practical wisdom, case studies, and habits* that will help you get the job of business-building done right, or at least better.

That self-awareness is the most critical factor for business-building and effective decision-making success is not a new insight. But the tougher code to crack, and what we emphasize ahead, is *how* to become more self-aware. To help frame this endeavor, we define four key business-builder character traits—Heart, Smarts, Guts, and Luck—and ask you to evaluate yourself against them to gauge where you are today and where you need to be tomorrow.

With awareness, you can begin improvement. Which brings us to purpose number two of the book: conveying important principles and practical tools that can be learned, honed, and practiced over time. We have tried to put forth a curated set of business lessons from our own experiences and those of the hundreds of entrepreneurs and business builders we interviewed. No business book, school, or mentor can guarantee success, but the combination of self-awareness and the right toolkit will certainly increase your odds.

So, who the heck are we? The three authors—Tony Tjan (that's me), Dick Harrington, and Tsun-yan Hsieh—come from backgrounds as entrepreneurs, large-company CEOs, consultants, and most recently as venture capitalists.

My own career has given me cause to reflect often on the forces that shape business success and failure. I grew up in the farthest-east point of Canada—in St. John's, Newfoundland—and I have always felt an entrepreneurial urge, beginning with the proverbial paper route in my preteen years. Things progressed from there to starting a small silkscreen T-shirt and sportswear venture (age thirteen), to selling imported picture frames door-to-door (age fifteen), to selling Apple II series computers for a local authorized dealer (age fifteen), and to being a distributor for a large multilevel-marketing skin care company (age seventeen). Throughout college, I continued doing things on the side. When I was accepted into Harvard Business School (HBS), some mentors and administrators there suggested that I try a more conventional job for a couple of years. So I deferred business school and in 1994 joined McKinsey & Co.'s Toronto office. That's where I met one of my most important and trusted mentors, my coauthor Tsun-yan Hsieh. Back to him in a bit.

Then I went to HBS, where with a few classmates and former McKinsey colleagues I founded a company called ZEFER, one of the earliest Internet advisory and development firms. (No, it's not an acronym; we just liked to capitalize all the letters.) It was 1997, and for a few years, ZEFER was a spectacular, unbelievable success. We raised money while we were still students, won the HBS business plan competition, raised a whole whack more dough, hired hundreds, and grew to more than $100 million in annual revenue. Then came the year 2000, and after the Internet bubble burst—right before our planned IPO—things went downhill fast. ZEFER lived (and lives) on as part of the Japanese conglomerate NEC, but back then it became clear that I had to move on to a new job. I did advisory work as a senior partner with The Parthenon Group—where I remain vice chairman—and separately as senior advisor to the CEO of the Thomson Corporation (none other than my coauthor Dick Harrington), before founding Cue Ball, the Boston-based venture capital firm where I work today.

One of Thomson's divisions was a ZEFER client, and it turned out Thomson was also a client of Parthenon's, which is how I first got to know Dick. At the time, Thomson was a diversified holding company that owned one of the world's biggest newspaper organizations. But Dick had other ideas.

Dick grew up in West Roxbury, Massachusetts—where he too had a newspaper route—and likes to joke about his "protracted" path to a degree at the University of Rhode Island, where he put his studies on hold to found and run a plumbing supply business. After graduation and a stint as an accountant, he worked through a variety of executive positions at Thomson, including head of its newspaper business. In 1997 he was named CEO, not long after which he made the shocking—and prescient—decision to start getting out of newspapers, as well as other noncore assets for the organization. Eventually, he would build and transform Thomson into what is today the world's largest information company, Thomson Reuters. I spent much of this time working very closely with Dick, and when he retired from Thomson Reuters in 2008 he joined me as partner and chairman of Cue Ball.

Now back to Tsun-yan. Dick and I were thrilled when Tsun-yan agreed to collaborate with us and be a coauthor because he brings not just a wealth of strategic wisdom but deep insights about leaders in context. Tsun-yan grew up in Singapore and spent thirty years, about half in North America and half in Asia and Europe, with McKinsey & Co. His leadership roles included chairman of McKinsey's Professional Development Committee, managing director of Canada, and managing director of its ASEAN practices. He mentored multiple generations of younger partners and associates, among whom several top leaders, including the current managing director of McKinsey, have emerged. Many of them turned to Tsun-yan for his counsel at pivotal career junctures. From these experiences, he has also seen and helped many others find inner resources to start or build a business. Today, Tsun-yan continues serving as a trusted counselor to company founders and CEOs across Asia and the Americas as founder of the Lin-Hart Group. In addition to directorship on the boards of global companies, he is a senior advisor and investor member of Cue Ball. Those who have worked with Tsun-yan use words such as "guru," "unsettling," "profound," and "mesmerizing." He is indeed a Yoda in the universe of strategists.

As Dick, Tsun-yan, and I began working on this project, we wanted to start by articulating a framework for successful business-building. We asked ourselves what were the most essential strengths of great entrepreneurs and builders of businesses. After many conversations among ourselves and with company founders and business leaders, the answer began to crystallize. Over lunch in Stamford, Connecticut, a couple of years ago, a former Thomson colleague asked, "What is it that really determines the success of businesspeople?" I started talking about some informal research we were doing and thoughts we had, then just blurted out, "You know, it really comes down to Smarts, Balls, and Luck." We were soon persuaded to go with *Guts* instead of *Balls* (our publisher said no way to the latter), and I introduced Smarts, Guts, and Luck as the core building blocks of the DNA of great entrepreneurs in a blog post for *Harvard Business Review Online* in March 2009.

As we did more research, reflection, and interviews, though, it became clear that another character trait needed to be included: Heart. Without Heart, few businesses ever become truly successful; passion and purpose are crucial instigators and guides. That brought us to *Heart, Smarts, Guts,* and *Luck,* or HSGL for short. Every entrepreneur and business-builder we know possesses every one of these four qualities, though the mix varies from person to person—and company founders lean toward one trait in particular (*hint:* it begins with H).

We call a person's unique mix of Heart, Smarts, Guts, and Luck an *HSGL profile,* and we've devised a survey, the Entrepreneurial Aptitude Test, to help you figure out what your profile looks like. There's a short version of this E.A.T. survey in chapter 10, and a complete survey online at the book's companion site, www.HSGL.com, which we encourage you to take. Throughout the book, we also share the results of an E.A.T. survey we conducted with approximately 350 entrepreneurs and business-builders, plus anecdotes and insights collected from dozens of interviews. There are more survey results, plus video interviews, at www.HSGL.com.

Figuring out which traits drive you and your decisions is the most important thing you can do to enhance your business leadership. Greater awareness of what you're best at, and how and when you might need to turn up or turn down the volume of the other traits, is what separates the best business-builders from those who are very good. From an organizational perspective, knowing your own HSGL profile allows you to better understand what kind of people best complement you during specific points of the business-building growth cycle—and, equally important, what type of person you might need to supplement (almost everyone needs a kindred spirit) or even succeed you.

An HSGL profile is akin to one's leadership personality. Just as a genetic screen can be an indicator of future health outcomes, so do the levels of your capabilities within each HSGL trait foreshadow prospective areas of triumph and trial during the business-building process. Are you ideally suited to starting a business, or to building and developing one? Do you see yourself as being the best, the biggest, or both? Are you self-aware enough to know when each of these qualities is relevant to a particular situation or growth phase? How does your profile impact how you interact with the team members you have today and those you will need tomorrow?

The E.A.T. survey does not tell you whether you have *enough* Heart, Smarts, Guts, or Luck to be successful in business. It is designed, like the psychometric tests that inspired it—Myers-Briggs Type Indicator, Predictive Index, and Relative Strength Index, among others—to suss out which traits are relatively stronger within you. This is very useful knowledge, but for true self-awareness you also need to have some sense of how you stack up in an absolute sense. We don't have a test for that, but many of the examples, questions, tools, and analyses in the book are meant to help you further think about—really think about—where you're strong and where you might fall short. Do you have what it takes to start a business? How genuine is your vision and purpose for that business? Do you recognize the likely future challenges and crossroads you'll face? What happens if you're below par in one of the four traits?

As you read this book, think about which parts resonate most with you and why. What parts seem more obvious and natural, and which passages a little more obtuse and challenging? It may be the latter that you want to focus on.

Businesses seldom test individuals or their leaders for self-awareness, and people seldom take the time to assess themselves. Yet self-awareness is not a soft organizational behavior concept to be dismissed. Rather it is the concrete foundation for improving your leadership and business-building capability. It is about intellectual honesty. It is about being aware of what you know and what you don't. It is key for spotlighting the areas where you could stand to improve and to know where another person's strengths could fit the bill better than your own.

Simply put: self-awareness motivates great business-builders to get better because they are better able to understand decisions they make.

With that in mind, chapters 1 through 5 explore the HSGL traits to help you build self-awareness. There's a chapter for each of the traits, and advice, exercises (including a few diagnostic True North questions), and stories along the way. Chapters 6 and 7 comprise two short chapters that discuss what to do with this awareness by exploring common (and less common) business-builder archetypes and how the different HSGL traits fit into different stages of the business growth cycle. The remainder of the book is all about practical wisdom, case studies, tools, and habits to help you move forward. The True North question sets in chapter 8 are meant to stimulate—you guessed it—self-awareness and also ignite debate, while the Wisdom Manifestos in chapter 9 amount to a "greatest hits" of business principles and frameworks that we have encountered in our research and in our careers. Finally, there's the abbreviated E.A.T. survey in chapter 10 and a wrap-up section with a few more interesting highlights and concluding thoughts.

Who is all this meant for? Given what we do for a living, we wrote the book with people planning to start, build, or run a business—or those already playing a key role in starting, building, or running something—in mind. But it's also meant to be useful for those in school or in some other job who are wondering whether entrepreneurship or business-building is right for them. Starting, running, and advising businesses has been an immensely fulfilling career—way of life, really—for all three of us. We'd love to convince more people to try it.

A Couple of Final Notes

We use the words *she* and *her* in our Heart and Smarts chapters and *he* and *him* in our chapters on Guts and Luck (and do a similar gender division among the business archetypes in chapter 6). We do this to dodge gender bias while staying on the right side of the laws of grammar.

Throughout this book, we use the terms *entrepreneurship* and *business-building*. They are related but different. *Entrepreneurship* refers to the first-stage founding of a business and connotes the classic Silicon Valley notion of a start-up and the innovative spirit required to launch one. In contrast, *business-building* is broader, encompassing the founding stages but also the growing, scaling, and extending of a business following its inception. Since entrepreneurs and business-builders often need to share similar traits, we sometimes use the terms interchangeably when describing the skills, habits, and characteristics of a successful individual.

Also, readers will note that this is *not* a traditional-looking business book. We wanted to make something digestible, practical, to the point— and fun to look at. We hope readers will not only find this a useful and timely read for their present-day initiatives, but also an ongoing reference guide that they'll mark up and dog-ear or even tear pages out of. We'd love nothing more than for our readers to actively read and cross-reference back and forth between pages, chapters, and our online resources. Of course, we welcome you to send us e-mails with questions or comments while or after you read this. Our most current contact information can always be found on this book's companion site, www.HSGL.com.

As business-builders turned advisors and venture capitalists, we applaud all of you who are already actively building businesses while trying to push yourselves to the next level. Not only are you the source of big ideas and innovations, you serve as an inspiration for all to continue pushing to our next level of potential. Coincidentally, as I prepare the final draft of this book's introduction for the publisher, a colleague e-mailed me a *Wikipedia* excerpt on one of the most expressed Greek values, *Areté*: "Translated as 'virtue,' the word actually means something closer to being the best you can be or reaching your highest human potential." We hope in its own small part that this book can help you toward that aspirational journey and goal.

—Anthony K. Tjan

1

TRAITS and PROFILES of GREAT ENTREPRENEURS

Heart, Smarts, Guts, and Luck are the defining traits of great entrepreneurs and business-builders. They are complementary in some ways, yet very different in others. We conclude this chapter with a visual depiction that puts the four traits in a nutshell (see figure 1-1).

The Heart-Dominant

With a three-act narrative bursting from their heads, Heart-dominant individuals bring purpose and passion to the business world. Founders, iconoclasts, and visionaries, their inspiration could be hard-core technology, e-commerce, hamburgers, rental cars, biotech, or a new take on social networking—it doesn't matter. These people are consumed by a deep passion and driving hunger to translate their purpose into reality.

We know at once when we're sitting across from a Heart-dominant person. Her passion for her idea is infectious, whether from her desire to get it just right or her voracious push to translate what she sees in her heart into words, and from there into a business that might just transform the world. Her approach may not always come across as rational. It may not be research-based. She may lack a conventional business plan. Tell her that her idea is crazy, poorly timed, or impossible, and she'll shrug or counter with all the reasons it will work. What matters to her is her desire to see her vision through.

Let's start with some nonbusiness (at least not conventional business) examples of Heart-dominant personalities. Chef Ferran Adrià of elBulli, a Catalan restaurant that was globally renowned for its mind-blowing take on molecular gastronomy, and Chez Panisse's Alice Waters, an advocate of fresh, sustainable ingredients, are two examples in the culinary world of Heart-dominant visionaries. Both aren't merely chefs, they're individuals committed to creating culinary movements. Their mission is to live their passion, share it with others, and leave a lasting mark.

Once we begin looking, the Heart-dominant individual shows up everywhere. The 2008 documentary *Man on Wire* portrayed French aerialist Philippe Petit, a man driven by the need to perform seemingly impossible feats—in this case, the 140-foot distance between New York's former World Trade Center twin towers. After months of planning, on August 7, 1974, Petit stepped out of the South Tower and onto a three-quarter-inch cable he had anchored between the towers the night before. He slowly began making his way back and forth from one tower to the other, 1,450 feet above the sidewalk. As we watched the documentary, we were at times unsure if we were watching fiction or reality. This is the genius and inspiration of the most Heart-dominant—they live with a willing suspension of disbelief and push us to new limits of possibility.

Consider the accordionist and street performer Guy Laliberté, who founded Cirque du Soleil and redefined the very meaning of "circus." Today Cirque du Soleil expects annual revenues of $1 billion.[1] Or Doris Christopher, a home-economics teacher and mother, who believed that every household should have professional-grade kitchen tools, and who created a contemporary "Tupperware party" organization of independent sales consultants bound together by a love of cooking. Doris dedicated her business, the Pampered Chef, to enhancing the quality of family life—a purpose-driven mission statement that may veer from the language of more traditional left-brain business types. But in 2002, Pampered Chef's yearly sales hit $700 million, and Berkshire Hathaway acquired the business.

The all-consuming, purposeful devotion of Heart-driven people ignites the most infectious pitches in the world of venture capital (it is hard not to be enthralled by someone else's genuine commitment to a cause). If you find yourself transfixed by someone who is talking about an idea, chances are you're in the presence of a Heart-dominant individual. Few truly successful businesses start without a Heart-dominant individual at their helm. Good ideas come from all types of people, but the Heart represents the richest soil that gives those initial ideas their roots. No, Heart alone isn't enough to accomplish great business-building, but it *is* a large part of what makes a company special. Without it, a venture often loses its meaning, purpose, and culture. In short, the Heart is the *why* to the *what* and *how* of business strategy.

The Smarts-Dominant

A Heart-dominant individual conjures up a great idea—a venture's seed or bulb. Typically, she has less interest in trying to understand the climate, soil type, or daily maintenance requirements. She will simply believe that the right things will happen and she will *will* the bulb to grow. Here the Smarts-dominant person comes in handy as a rational, fact-driven force who begins steering the business by delegating and setting goals, forging a system of accountability, articulating strategy, and emphasizing top-notch performance. To stick with the garden analogy, a Smarts-dominant person pores over the *Farmer's Almanac*, carefully optimizes the fertilizers, and ensures that the bulb is watered on an appropriate schedule.

It is important to note that Smarts is multidimensional. We have in our experiences observed different types, ranging from the stereotypical Book Smarts, to People Smarts, Street Smarts, and Creative Smarts. Cutting across all these types of Smarts is a capacity for *pattern recognition*. The ability to absorb and classify patterns through trial and error, business experience, handy shortcuts gleaned from a university seminar, or sheer shrewdness about human behavior leads to practical, repeatable habits that in time become second nature and apply directly to successful business-building. It is pattern recognition, therefore, that we see as the defining quality of business smarts.

As companies mature, leaders need to scale and develop institutional processes so that their businesses can sustain themselves. The Smarts-dominant individual may not have come up with the core business idea, but she has a rare ability to seize, capture, frame, and extend its essence. She connects ideas, trends, and patterns earlier and faster than others and then shapes them into a coherent storyline. Where others may see chaos, she uses logic, perception, critical intelligence, experience, and a gut knowledge of markets and conditions to propel a business forward. If the Heart-dominant person kicks things off with passion and fire, the Smarts-dominant individual is best suited to providing structure, analysis, and a pragmatic and actionable plan, Her job is not to smother or defuse the founder's vision, but to ground, extend, and expand it.

Smarts-dominant individuals can be highly successful business-builders. Meg Whitman at eBay and Jeff Bezos at Amazon are both good examples. Whitman built her first career as a consultant at Bain & Company, while Jeff Bezos forged a career at D. E. Shaw, a New York investment firm. Bezos did not grow up toiling in the book industry, but instead saw a great opportunity in the growth of the Internet, and then methodically reviewed the top mail-order businesses to pinpoint which ones might flourish on the Web. Unlike a Heart-dominant individual, the Smarts-dominant person might first establish key facts to drive her decision: *What is the largest market out there? Where are the black holes? What is our blue ocean strategy?*

That said, pure brain-based IQ is perhaps the *least* essential quality for business success. The most outstanding entrepreneurs and business-builders across the globe generally possess as much or more Street, People, and Creative Smarts. Most people already have the minimum of IQ/Book Smarts requisite to build a business, but overemphasize its importance.

The Guts-Dominant

It takes guts to act, accept a risk, and to try something new. If the world were full of passionate and purposeful people with brilliant minds, but no Guts to act, there would be no progress. We might still be living in hovels and trying to catch fish with pointy sticks. This is why we need Guts-dominant people, who are all about starting and sustaining action.

The Guts trait can be subdivided in several different ways. One is the divide between risk *takers* and risk *tolerators*. Risk takers derive excitement and engagement from being in a situation laden with meaningful uncertainty. Many of the entrepreneurs we have spoken to refer to the dramatic emotional shifts of their "high-amplitude" lives (they love it that way, too). Bungee jumpers, cliff divers, and other adrenaline junkies are extreme examples of Guts-dominant people. So too are entrepreneurs and innovators trying to break into new fields, as are financiers and executives who seek to turn around mismanaged or poorly performing companies. Or they are people who are just uneasy with a five-year plan and crave a sense of adventure to make each day matter.

Risk tolerators do not necessarily seek risk, yet willingly pursue their goals by understanding and accepting and managing the risks inherent in a given decision. The Guts-oriented professionals we spoke to, such as doctor and former astronaut Scott Parazynski, are risk tolerators. The common correlation between astronauts, entrepreneurs, and high-performance athletes, Parazynski told us, is one of understanding and assessing the risks at hand and learning how best to mitigate them.[2] These risk-tolerant individuals confront fear not with the risk-seeker's defiant smile but with thoughtful training, management, and self-awareness techniques.

Another way to slice up Guts (not the most pleasant image, we admit) is between (1) the Guts to Initiate, (2) the Guts to Endure and (3) the Guts to Evolve. This maps to the growth of a business. Entrepreneurs need to initiate with conviction, but for most businesses the bigger test lies in preserving (Guts to Endure). For those businesses that finally achieve a steady state of success, the next challenge becomes having the Guts to Evolve, often into something different than what made you successful in the beginning.

Guts also reveals itself over different time frames as *longitudinal* or *episodic*. The longitudinal type of guts requires resilience and perseverance. The late Swedish journalist Stieg Larsson wrote three volumes of what he hoped someday would be a ten-part series without having first secured a publisher. They became huge global bestsellers—albeit after his death. Ralph Lauren, the Bronx-born teenaged son of Ashkenazi Jews from Belarus, sold neckties to his classmates in middle school and worked after school to buy suits, and parlayed his vision and resilience into a business with 2011 revenues of $5.6 billion. The crowning example of longitudinal Guts may well be Nelson Mandela, who spent twenty-seven years as a political prisoner and then, four years after his release, was elected president of South Africa. Every one of these larger-than-life figures demonstrated guts over the long term. Each dealt with setbacks, solitude, derision, uncertainty, and opposition.

The Guts we term *episodic* is about making tough-but-right decisions on your feet, often at a moment of truth. A Guts-dominant person shows what he's made of when crisis times ask him to react quickly and conclusively. Guts shows its face at those moments when a company announces layoffs, when a potential Bill Gates or Mark Zuckerberg drops out of Harvard to follow his dream, or when a business-builder commits to hiring people despite knowing he might not make payroll unless a contract that's currently pending comes through. Military leaders have long defined Guts not as blind fearlessness, but as the ability to put fear into perspective. "All men are frightened," General George S. Patton once said. "The more intelligent they are, the more they are frightened. The courageous man is the man who forces himself, in spite of his fear, to carry on." We couldn't have said it better ourselves.

In the business world, it takes Guts at every growth phase and threshold. Pick your analogy: learning to fly while you're building a plane; jumping off a cliff while hoping to grab a parachute along the way; driving cross-country with the lights off. Guts makes for a similar bullheaded conviction in the face of uncertainty.

The Luck-Dominant

Luck is present to some extent in just about all business-builders, even those who are not primarily driven by it. Almost everyone, after all, has realized an advantage that was just plain Lucky. In its commonly understood form, Luck feels random, chaotic, selective, arbitrary, and seemingly beyond our control. We can't cook, conjure, or dream it into being.

We *can*, however, become more receptive to Luck and in some cases even influence it. Here's an observation that became clear in our research: at its core, most Luck is the result of a Lucky Attitude and a Lucky Network. Luck-oriented people maintain an attitude based on humility conjoined with two other factors—intellectual curiosity and optimism. This three-part formulation helps beget a Lucky Network. Very different from a traditional set of "important" contacts, a Lucky Network is a subset of your overall network. It is an idiosyncratic amalgam of authentic relationships with folks who might not appear to be especially "strategic" or "valuable" but who over time become so. In addition to the Lucky Attitude, this organic process of cultivating a Lucky Network is enhanced by the four characteristics of vulnerability, authenticity, generosity, and openness.

Acknowledging the part Luck plays in life isn't easy for most people. It's tempting to take full credit for our own successes, especially if we've had a few. Giving credit to the role Luck plays in our careers obliges us to accept that we have less control over what happens in our lives than most of us want to admit.

If you scan the biography of any successful entrepreneur, chances are good you will find at least one moment, meeting, turning point, or convergence of people, places, or things, that altered that person's business or career path. That's Luck, and it comes in three varieties: Dumb, Constitutional, or Circumstantial. Although you cannot alter Dumb Luck, and can do very little about Constitutional Luck, we strongly believe you can work toward creating or strengthening Circumstantial Luck.

Circumstantial Luck occurs when you're dining with a friend who bumps into a friend . . . who then somehow ends up becoming one of your most important clients. None of this would have happened if he hadn't chosen that particular lunch date or restaurant, or if that third party hadn't shown up at just the right moment. The Luck here was derived from the confluence of several different circumstances—including attitude and relationship network—aligning toward a positive outcome.

So, how can you make yourself luckier?

First, no matter how powerful and successful they become, Luck-oriented individuals retain a measure of humility. All of us have chance encounters, but lucky people are humble enough to believe that they have to seize these encounters as they happen, as if the world won't easily offer up such opportunities again.

Second, Luck-oriented people, as a response to their humility, are driven by a profound intellectual curiosity. Again and again, they question the norm. They read, explore, reframe, discuss, argue, sample, and discard, all with an internal resolve to better themselves and challenge their own and others' perspectives. This eagerness to question their surroundings increases the likelihood that they can grab an opportunity as it swoops past. Was Alice lucky to find Wonderland, or was she curious and open enough to follow the White Rabbit? In the end, wasn't it one and the same?

Third and most important, Luck-oriented people have an optimism that is the source of the energy and belief that turn intellectual thirst into reality. Because they *believe* that great things can happen, they pursue such endeavors. In general, they are givers of energy rather than takers of it.

Indeed, Heart-Luck is a combination profile common among founders. How we perceive our own luckiness also tends to become a self-fulfilling prophecy.

Consider Laurel Touby, a journalist turned accidental Internet entrepreneur. "I don't know if anybody would have said 'Laurel's going to be an entrepreneur,' or 'Laurel's going to be a writer,' or 'Laurel's going to be anything,'"[3] she recalls. In 1994, Touby started having cocktail parties and mixers in her apartment in an effort to have people in the media industry meet and try to help each other. In her own words, she never conceived of that becoming a business. But she began asking guests to pay $100 *if* they found the service useful—that is, to pay on a volunteer basis. This grew into Mediabistro, which was started in 1994 and went online in 1996—one of the earliest job-posting sites. Sold to Jupitermedia in 2007 for $23 million, Mediabistro has evolved into an online destination for media professionals looking for jobs, events, courses, contacts, and information. Much of Touby's success stemmed from her honesty about the many aspects of the business she did not know, and her optimism that circumstances or relationships would help her with what she needed. She had many of the other HSGL traits going for her, but attitude and relationships created the

FIGURE 1-1

HSGL Traits in Summary

	HEART ♥	SMARTS	GUTS	LUCK ♣
Code for	**Authentic Vision** • Purpose • Passion • Sacrifice • Nuance	**Pattern Recognition** Business Smarts = Book Smarts + Street Smarts + People Smarts + Creative Smarts	**Types of Guts** • Guts to Initiate • Guts to Endure • Guts to Evolve	**Lucky Attitude** • Humility • Intellectual curiosity • Optimism **Lucky Network**
Exemplified by	• Alice Waters, Chef • Guy Laliberté, Cirque du Soleil • Howard Schultz, Starbucks	• Jeff Bezos, Amazon • Bob Langer, MIT	• Nelson Mandela • Richard Branson, Virgin Airlines • Paul Reichmann, Olympia & York	• Jay Chiat, TBWA\Chiat\Day • Li Lu, Coleader, Tiananmen Square 1989
Showcased in/ analogs	• Philippe Petit in *Man on Wire* • John Keating in *Dead Poets Society*	• Will Hunting in *Good Will Hunting* • Frank Abagnale in *Catch Me if You Can*	• King George VI in *The King's Speech* • Harvey Milk in *Milk*	• Jamal in *Slumdog Millionaire* • Forrest Gump in *Forrest Gump*

right type of circumstance for Luck to come her way and her determination took full advantage of it. The combination of a Lucky Attitude with a Lucky Network proved exceptionally powerful for her.

So, in our view, what we often brush away as "dumb luck" is, in fact, Circumstantial Luck that is more a function of the right attitude and the right relationship network. Thus, while there can be no doubt that some, well, "luck" is involved in being lucky, Luck-oriented individuals are that way because of their attitude of humility, intellectual curiosity, and optimism that conspire with one's relationships to coax out of the universe positive forces and events.

2

❤ HEART:
Winning WITH THE Heart

Is a business plan always necessary? Actually, it may be detrimental, especially at the beginning of company creation (the conception stage when most people believe they need a business plan the most). The best businesses are less likely to have started with a business plan than they are by founders who jumped into the fray and just started *doing*. In the course of our research, we asked entrepreneurs across the globe how they launched their businesses. Of those who had successful exits, nearly 70 percent did *not* start with a business plan. These successful businesses kicked off far less formulaically, with a quality we call *Heart*.

Too often, aspiring entrepreneurs over think how they should launch a business. *What is the exact market size of the opportunity?* they ask themselves. *What is my projected first-year share of the market? What is the pro forma five-year financial plan?* Although questions such as these can be helpful if approached as approximations, they often deliver answers that are "precisely incorrect" (meaning very, very detailed work that completely misses the mark). From our perspective, there are times in a business life cycle where the right call to action and the right type of "research" is to "Just Nike It"—that is, to *just do it*—to start, iterate, evolve, then use these experiences as the research input to begin formulating a plan. Heart-dominant individuals are far more likely to take this path. (Later in this chapter, "Do

You Really Have Your Heart in Your Business?" offers a set of True North questions you can use to help evaluate the Heart in your business.)

70 percent of founders with a successful exit started without a plan.

MBAs often spend considerable time looking *outside* themselves for an idea that would make for a good plan, versus looking *inside* themselves for the purpose and passion that might underlie a great vision. That is the difference between a true-blue founder and someone who is seeking to become a founder. As we will see, the markets also recognize this distinction, and end up disproportionately rewarding the starters of businesses—that is, the real founders. The founders who start, execute, and win on big ideas are seldom those who have methodically planned their way. Instead, their Heart gives birth to an idea and a culture. Founders tend to start through an iterative set of tests of their ideas. Passionate trial and error is more the order of the day than spreadsheets and erudite reflections. Larry Page, the cofounder and CEO of Google, has said that there are no good slow decisions, only good fast decisions.

Of our four business-building traits of Heart, Smarts, Guts, and Luck, Heart is perhaps the most challenging to define. To both new and expe-

Heart Defined

Heart \hahrt\ *noun* 1 : the source of an authentic vision and the soul of a business or calling

How Heart Reveals Itself

Purpose and Passion + *Sacrifice / Work Ethic* + *Nuance*

rienced business-builders, it risks coming across as ephemeral and soft. Which is ironic, as Heart may be the most critical distinguishing feature between people who have successfully started companies and those who choose to be part of another person's vision. We're reminded of our informal canvassing of alumni from top MBA programs. When asked which courses have had the most subsequent impact on their lives, most name an organizational behavior or leadership class. What can seem and feel soft in the moment becomes real and powerful over time.

Three distinguishing traits characterize the Heart-driven individual:

1. Purpose (and the passion that comes with it): You cannot plan Heart, or "in vitro fertilize" a truly great business. A company's foundation lies in its purpose.

2. Sacrifice and *agape*: The concept of *agape* (defined later in this chapter) and the natural maternal-like sacrifice that comes with creating and building a business.

3. Nuance: The subtleties and thousand points of light that emanate and coalesce from a genuine Heart and ultimately differentiate it from its competitors.

Let's delve into each dimension that defines Heart.

Purpose and Passion

The foundational qualities of Heart—purpose and passion—are neither innately born nor externally learned. They come from *both* nature and nurture. But frankly, it doesn't matter whether you were born with a calling and passion to do something or if you were exposed to a calling or passion through parents, teachers, mentors, schooling, great books, or travel. Heart is about what you purposely, passionately, and insanely love doing, period. Nature and nurture lead you to a place where you intuit a purpose and a passion to change the way things are done.

So what might be your purpose and passion? Consider these questions:

- What is the thing you do naturally better and that you care more about than others do?

- How do you enjoy spending your leisure time?

- If you had all the money in the world, what would you be doing?

Over the years, some business school students have shown up in our offices saying, "I have a ten-year plan toward becoming an entrepreneur." Really? A ten-year plan to become an entrepreneur? What's that about?

Among the reasons they give for their "deferred entrepreneurship":

> "I want to spend some years learning first and building a base of security."

> "I don't have access to the capital or resources to start."

> "I know I want to be an entrepreneur; I just don't have the ideas."

Make no mistake, these are all rational reasons. But entrepreneurship isn't something you rationally plot, devise, schedule, reschedule, or delay. To say that you feel that you are an entrepreneur but just don't have an idea is akin to saying that you are a chef but don't know which meals you want to cook. Planning for an idea is next to impossible. You simply can't in vitro fertilize a great business. Which is why Heart-driven entrepreneurs are fundamentally different from the rest of the population. Heart-driven founders connect with a passion and a purpose deep down inside. They are inspired by everything they touch, see, do, and hear. They are unconventionally idealistic. They carry a different risk profile. They don't tie themselves up into knots about security—the term itself often makes them uneasy. (Many entrepreneurs find the need to do it again and again, to the point of risking their newfound security, as the notion of comfort rubs them the wrong way.)

You cannot "in vitro fertilize" a great business.

Harvard Business School professor Bill Sahlman defines entrepreneurship as "the relentless pursuit of opportunity without regard to resources."[1]

A Heart-driven person cares less about what she lacks and more about what she can achieve with what she already has. She may not know what the future holds, but she forges ahead anyway. Take a moment to reflect on a handful of iconoclastic founders: Richard Branson (going from the music business to launching an airline, then a space-travel initiative), Steve Jobs (making design and experience a competitive advantage en route to transforming Apple into a media company), or any one of several entrepreneurs

Labor of Love

"Vimeo was a labor of love. Of all the ideas that I can apply myself to, I filter out the ones I could love, and then I further filter out the ones that I could sustain."[2]

Zach Klein's Entrepreneurial DNA

PERCENT OF TOTAL (ADDS TO 100%)

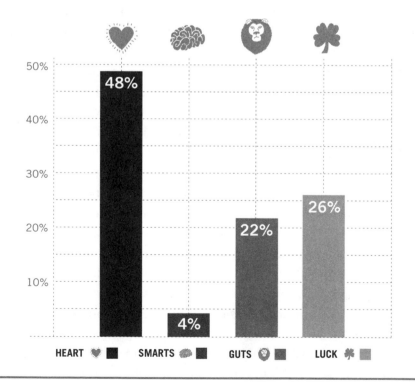

HEART 48% SMARTS 4% GUTS 22% LUCK 26%

in Warren Buffett's Berkshire Hathaway stable, including Doris Christopher of Pampered Chef, and—one of Buffett's favorite case studies—Rose Blumkin, the founder of Nebraska Furniture Mart, who started her business with a $500 loan and the motto "Sell Cheap and Tell the Truth." Each of these founders brought purpose, passion, and a deep love affair to their initiatives (see the sidebar from Zach Klein on this). In short, they all have, or had, incredible Heart.

The Power of Purpose and Passion

The drive, movement, and contagiousness of a business derive from its purpose and passion, which are typically a reflection of the founder's Heart. Before doing anything else, at the onset of company creation, founders need to generate widespread energy and inspiration. Purpose should always come before company, product, and profit, especially during a business's early stages.

Mats Lederhausen, a partner of Dick and Tony's at Cue Ball, has spent years mulling over the power of purpose. Heart and purpose are nearly synonymous but not quite; the second follows closely from the first. Both point to the necessity of launching a business by addressing the *why* before the *how* and the *what*. Or, as Mats likes to say, "Purpose before product, and product before profit." To translate, the root of a great business is purpose—understanding fully why you are doing what you are doing and grasping its meaning to you as an individual and its larger meaning to society.

Mats says purpose does not need to equate to nonprofit or social entrepreneurship. By his definition, purpose is about thinking explicitly of how you can change the world for the better and create businesses with integrity, on a values-driven system. *Would people miss this business if it went away tomorrow?* is a good litmus test of a purposeful business.

Think of companies like Ikea, Patagonia, Nike, or Southwest Airlines. Their purposes are palpable and, yes, we would miss all four if they disappeared overnight. Ikea's purpose is to democratize design for the masses by selling affordable furniture. Patagonia is a pioneer in responsible manufacturing, conservation, and sustainability. Nike's purpose has less to do with sneakers and more to do with getting into the game and embracing activity. When you visit Nike's Oregon headquarters, it's like being in a gym: it exudes "active lifestyle." And then there is Southwest, the little airline that could. Fun, idiosyncratic, and even a little nutty, the airline is about seeking and savoring freedom, and allowing people to "spread their wings." Each one of these businesses can be said to bring an authenticity of purpose and passion that brings an immeasurable power to their brands.

As a business grows, founders eventually need to refocus their attention on balancing company culture with structure and process. But if they begin structuring things too early, they will sacrifice whatever opportunity they had to architect and articulate their company's soul and mission; in short, they will begin by managing a company they have not yet led. To be clear, eventually the shift of focus (as we will discuss in chapters 6 and 7) needs to be about how core aspects of the Heart and its purpose can be institutionalized for the future. Maintaining the purpose and in effect soul of a company is perhaps one of the greatest leadership challenges. Think of Sony under cofounder Akio Morita versus some of the more recent and more difficult periods in that company's history. Or fast-forward to the present and consider the challenge for Apple to preserve core elements of what Steve Jobs provided, but also dare to evolve differently in a post-Jobs world with the understanding that replication would be impossible.

> Be careful not to begin managing a company that has not yet been led.

Figure 2-1, a chart from Mats Lederhausen, illustrates a key point: purpose at the beginning of a venture has a huge impact on who you are. Everything else should emanate from, or reinforce, that purpose (see his comments in "Mats Lederhausen on Purpose Bigger Than Product").[3]

The Greatest Love Requires Sacrifice

Genuinely Heart-dominant founders and business-builders focus less on burning, short-lived attractions and concepts, and embody instead what

FIGURE 2-1

Power and Impact of Purpose: The Starting Point of Great Businesses

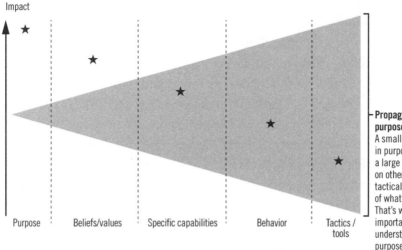

How to read this chart: The dots represent the impact (Y-axis) of each aspect of a business. The shaded area shows how a change in purpose can have big effects on other parts of the business.

the ancient Greeks called the *love of sacrifice*: they stick with the core of their idea and make sacrifices to see it through. The second part of Heart's definition has to do with this sacrifice.

Democracy, architecture, and steam baths weren't the only lasting contributions the classical Greeks left behind. Between cultivating olives and carving marble columns, they also found time to define (at least) three varieties of "love." You're probably familiar with *eros* (ἔρως), which came to refer to sensual love, and *philia* (φιλία), which denotes a profound friendship or loyalty. But the Greeks also recognized a third category of love known as *agape* (ἀγαπη), the expression of love between parents and their children, or between leaders and the people they serve. The King James Bible (1 Corinthians 13) describes *agape* as "sacrificial love," while other sources alternately define it as divine, unconditional, and all-encompassing. Just as parents often sacrifice their wants and needs for their children, Heart-dominant entrepreneurs typically shelve their own personal comforts and needs in order to make their businesses succeed. For Heart-dominant entrepreneurs, great concepts are akin to children,

Mats Lederhausen on Purpose Bigger Than Product

Mats Lederhausen began his career as a teenager behind the cash register of a McDonald's and in time became owner-operator of more than 150 franchises. Ultimately, he led McDonald's worldwide strategy, and became managing director of McDonald's Ventures, where he grew highly successful concepts such as Pret A Manger, Chipotle, and RedBox.

What is your philosophy of "purpose bigger than product" all about?

At its core, it's about driving from the Heart and about being real. In business, trust and authenticity are perhaps the most important currencies. Businesses and consumers should be connected through the same hymn. Some people dub that hymn *vision*; and you as authors are dubbing it in some ways as Heart. I call it *purpose*. All these words mean essentially the same thing. Each one answers the central questions: *Why are you here? Why are you doing what you are doing, and why might it matter?*

If you conceive of your purpose as fuzzy, your business design will invariably suffer. On the other hand, if you have a sharp conception of your purpose, of your Heart, and what footprints you want to leave, your design will be pure in expressing and reinforcing that purpose.

How can a company lead with purpose?

Purpose is about what you do more than what you say or tell your employees and customers. This is what makes ideas believable. And of course, ideas have to be believable. They can't be pipe dreams. As John Naisbitt once said: "You can't get so far ahead of the parade that no one knows you're in it."

---

which is why a colleague once coined the expression *pregnancy envy* for entrepreneurs.

Narayana Murthy, founder of Infosys, the Indian software-services giant, tells the story of how his children related to his company:

It was on one of those rare nights at home during the late eighties. I was huddling with my young children, Rohan and Akshata, when Rohan, the most mischievous child I have ever come across, asked innocently whether I loved Infosys more than him and his sister. I got away from that embarrassing situation by saying that I loved my children much more than anything else. However, even today when we reminisce about the incident, my children are not fully convinced that I was telling them the truth. When I was spending sixteen-hour days in the office and was away from home for as many as 330 days in a year, it was hard for my children to believe in my commitment to the family.[4]

The maternal need and desire to give birth to an idea, and the willingness to make whatever sacrifices are necessary to turn that idea into a reality and nurture it through its growth, is the business-building corollary of *agape*, or sacrificial love. This trait propels entrepreneurs to spend long nights fine-tuning prototypes, lecturing everyone within earshot about the unappreciated details of the perfect customer experience, and spending consecutive all-nighters coding to ensure a better release. For the founders of the best and most successful start-ups, this *agape* is the motivating fuel for hard work. Not surprisingly, it's always about hard work—really hard work!—and deliberate trade-offs. Having fun or making friends is a distant second on the list. Yet because Heart-dominant entrepreneurs are genuinely purpose-driven and passion-driven about their ideas, their sacrifices never feel burdensome.

In sacrifice they often find mastery. In research popularized in Malcolm Gladwell's *Outliers*, Professor K. Anders Ericsson of Florida State University's Psychology Department found that approximately ten thousand hours of deliberate practice—which translates into approximately three hours of goal-oriented practice daily for a decade—generally yields world-class expertise. Via their iterations and desire to fulfill their purpose, most entrepreneurs exceed three hours of deliberate practice a day. Like the pianist looking to perfect her technique or repertoire, entrepreneurs seek to become maestros in their own areas of business creation.

That success comes from unrelenting hard work and dedication should come as a relief to many. The "natural-born" CEO is less common than someone who works tirelessly to realize her underlying potential. But it is only when the Heart's natural and authentic passion for the purpose underlying the idea kicks in that the intensity of the drive and work ethic

The Heart to Sacrifice

"I was working many hours, but I was working out of
a love and addiction for building companies."[5]

David Hornik's Entrepreneurial DNA

Percent of total (adds to 100%)

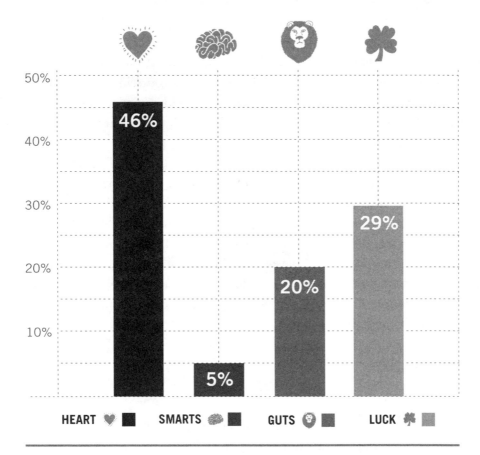

seem worth it. (After all, many people work hard—but aren't fully engaged
with the purpose of the company where they work.)

As Tsun-yan says, Heart, and its quality of *agape*, mean simply that *we
care enough to put aside other things to devote ourselves indefinitely to our
dream*. Nothing motivates us more, or compels us to work harder, than a

compelling or infectious idea. In our experience, few individuals wish to disrupt the status quo, whereas the greatest business-builders want nothing more than to bust open whatever ceilings stand in their way. Heart drives both *distance*—the endurance and hard work over time that success requires—as well as those bursts of productivity, which we dub *height*. Heart, and the hard work it requires, is thus characteristic of both the marathoner and the sprinter, often within the same race. If we approach an idea or business with Heart, hard work not only becomes tolerable, it turns into a fierce exercise in headlong joy. Many people make the mistake of confusing Heart with strenuous effort. While greater purpose behind an idea motivates harder work, merely working harder at something does not create passion. If you find your effort flagging, ask yourself: *Was your Heart genuine in the first place?* In this sense, you should anticipate the sacrifice Heart makes toward business-building to the point where it feels like the natural thing to do.

"There came a time in 1990 when we were floundering," remembered Narayana Murthy of Infosys. "We had offers to buy us out which my colleagues thought we should consider, since we weren't making too much headway. We had a four- to five-hour discussion, and I could feel the sense of despondency. So I said, 'Guys, don't worry, I'll buy you out. I know it's going to be tough . . . but I have no doubt that we'll see light.' In minutes, they all said, 'We're with you. From now onward we will never discuss the issue of closing down, getting tired, or giving up. This marathon will be restarted.'"

Nuance, or Every Little Thing Counts

This third part of Heart is less tangible and intuitive than the first two elements of purpose and sacrifice. It's *nuance*.

What does it take to be uniquely the best at something? The answer lies in nuance. In the case of great entrepreneurs, business-builders, and other iconoclasts, nuance stems from an undisguised authenticity (from the Heart), mixed with the capacity to discern and express what would otherwise be imperceptible. The Heart-led nuance of iconoclasts such as Alice Waters, Steve Jobs, or Ralph Lauren derives not from the 99 percent of items that can be functionally learned and perfected by others through time, but rather from the remaining 1 percent that no one else can replicate. Which is as good a translation of nuance as any: those subtle, barely discernible differences that are virtually impossible to see, but that can be disproportionately *felt*.

In business, nuance is that "something" or "pixie dust" that creates the unique differentiation of a business, a product, or a brand. Consider a symphonic score played by two different orchestras, both performed to technical perfection but one coming across, somehow, as tonally different, more soulful, more *connected*. Or think about the ability of some wine connoisseurs to perceive on a blind basis the differences between a vertical of wine (a series of the same wine from different vintages).

By definition, nuance is subtle; it generally refers to near-inaudible emphases and minute changes of expression or meaning. We have emphasized that great businesses need to be driven at the outset, cardinally, by an instigating purpose and passion-driven Heart. But the authenticity of the Heart derives not just from the clarity of its big-picture purpose but from all of its imperfect, incomplete, genuine, unpolished, and raw elements—that is, from its nuance. The nuance that Heart then creates is a collective of small but essential things, or quirks, that not only make a company special and immediately identifiable, but helps sustain its competitive difference over the long run.

Though you will probably never find the word *nuance* in any business plan, this delicate third definitional element of the Heart creates the potential for beloved brands and great businesses.

Among the nuances Apple offers is the convergence of design and functionality, perfectly mirrored by the late Jay Chiat's iconic "Think Different" ad campaign, which injected a knowing, minimalist tone that was and still is in sync with the company's operating culture. Food retailer Trader Joe's conveys nuance via its quirky operating culture, ambassadorial staff, sense of belonging, and the local references of its in-store signage. A nuance of spirit and purpose contributes to the success of Ikea, where customers participate in the selection, pick-up, and construction of ready-to-assemble, flat-pack furniture—while following a walking path that leads them into a restaurant where they can eat meatballs with lingonberries. Nuance can transform a simple functional transaction into an emotional experience.

As the best companies evolve, they continually improve, enhance, and tweak even the tiniest details that make up their purpose. The most subtle angle of a product, the specific and deliberate blending of two unusual Pantone hues, or the slightest shift of a tiny part of a homepage's user interface are among the elements that great founders and business-builders know can make a difference. Nuance drives long-term differentiation for a business, but also continually resets the bar for differentiation. This is because savvy customers come to appreciate the nuances once they see them, and expect more once they have experienced what is possible.

In the case of one of our venture firm's own portfolio investments—Epic Burger, a natural burger chain—we have watched over the years as founder David Friedman maniacally focused on the smallest details and nuances, his goal being to create the most perfect and "mindful" burger in the world. How might the bun-to-meat ratio (in terms of size) improve? Which pickles, and in what shape and size, delivered the optimal "flavor profile" for his burger? Which potato gave the best flavor for the hand-cut fries, and did they complement the taste of the burger? What kind of ketchup? What kind of salt? How should the environment enhance the food experience; what decor should be changed? Should he alter the line locations to speed up order taking? Should he add another register? What about the menu design? Could it be made simpler? The list goes on. For any entity that has its eye on large-scale success, perfecting the offering at the smallest level first before scaling is critical.

During a company's early days, there is little time to gain consensus on everything, and people naturally respond to a leader with a strong vision and strong Heart. In those early days and beyond, the authentic, purpose-filled, passionate story that the founder tells creates contagion across a business, while over time, the third dimension of the Heart, nuance, serves as an ongoing inspiration to give the business its differentiation, its uniqueness, and a lot of its soul.

Carried out properly, nuance, character, and connectivity can transform consumers into engaged, interactive participants who "belong" to your company's story. The power of nuance is why we encourage Heart-dominant founders to embrace their own idiosyncrasies, as well as the unconventional nuances of their concepts. Heart comes in all shapes, sizes, and refinements. Yes, there is a fine line between whimsical and trivial, but aren't the businesses we love as quirky, authentic, and true to themselves, faults and all, as the people we love? Nuance is a beautiful thing and when all of the nuances of a business converge, everyone knows it and feels it.

What the Heart Is Not

There is often confusion between short-lived infatuation and whims and genuine callings of the Heart. There is a fundamental difference between Heart and lust.

Heart Is Not Lust

Anyone can become smitten, or fall in "lust," with an alluring business idea. So let's take a moment to distinguish between lust and the authentic passion that comes with Heart.

We use the term *lustful* to describe those who chase after the hottest trends of the minute. With every market, technological, economic, or cultural shift—social networking, hedge funds, distressed assets, green-tech, clean-tech, consumer web, and so forth—comes any number of lust-driven "entrepreneurs" who are more opportunistic and excited about making money than they are genuinely passionate about pursuing the underlying ideas and innovation behind those trends. Value *capture* is not the same as value *creation*.

We serve as perennial judges for various business-plan competitions, and every week Dick and Tony review multiple plans for prospective investment. From an investment standpoint, we have a natural preference for businesses that are on trend and part of a rising tide. At the same time, we look somewhat askance at in-lust "trend-surfers" who don't fully understand, or connect with, the true business zeitgeist. As a cynic once remarked, and we paraphrase, *To make money, consider shorting a graduating class of any top business school for its first few years out as its members belatedly chase what is "hot."* One critical venture capital guideline and lesson we believe in strongly and even live by is this: people always trump ideas. Trends and plans inevitably change, so before all else, consider the person behind the concept. We continually seek out the authentically purposeful, passionate Heart-driven entrepreneur who wants to create a lasting business.

Heart Cannot Be Defined by Hard Work Alone

Heart's secondary trait, which we defined as sacrifice and *agape*, should not be confused with just plain hard work. *Agape* is tied to an almost maternal quality of sacrifice, where a founder's love and passion for the business and its underlying idea drives the hard work. Many professional careers demand hard work. Many of us may remember hundred-plus-hour weeks from earlier in our careers, but hundred-plus-hour weeks do not necessarily equate with being Heart-driven! Ask someone if they want to work hard and they will usually answer that they are happy to work hard on behalf of something they believe in strongly. People will usually either become resentful or indifferent to jobs that require sacrifice without the intrinsic reward of a meaningful role and larger purpose. On the other hand, people can accept the trade-off of hard work when it is on behalf of something they care about, something that makes a difference to them personally and to the rest of society.

Founders—the Ultimate Torchbearers of Heart

Of all the different types and stages of business-builders, it comes as no surprise to learn that *founders* are the most Heart-driven people out there. It doesn't take long to figure out who might be a great entrepreneurial founder. You know a true founder when you see it. (In fact, you *feel* it.) Entrepreneurial ardor—the fire in the belly—is both exhilarating and contagious. Founders are highly biased in their decision-making actions toward being Heart-dominant, and at the core of Heart-driven individuals is deep passion. By extension, high-Heart individuals tend to be most fired up either at the start of businesses or at restart points (i.e., when growth has stalled). Fueled by purpose and hunger, founders with strong Heart characteristics are compelled not only to build a business but to share their mission and vision with the rest of the world.

60 percent of founders are Heart-driven.

Google cofounder Sergey Brin told us that of all the HSGL traits, "I'd probably rank Heart—the passion for something and the desire to see it through, no matter what the challenge—as number one."[6] Adds Kimbal

FIGURE 2-2

The Market Rewards the Efforts of Founders

Forbes 100 wealthiest people in America

55 FOUNDERS	31 CEOs/ EXECUTIVES	14 INHERITORS

Among the top, founders amass greater wealth

FOUNDERS: $478 BILLION	CEOs/ EXECUTIVES: $92 BILLION
————— 84% —————	—16%—

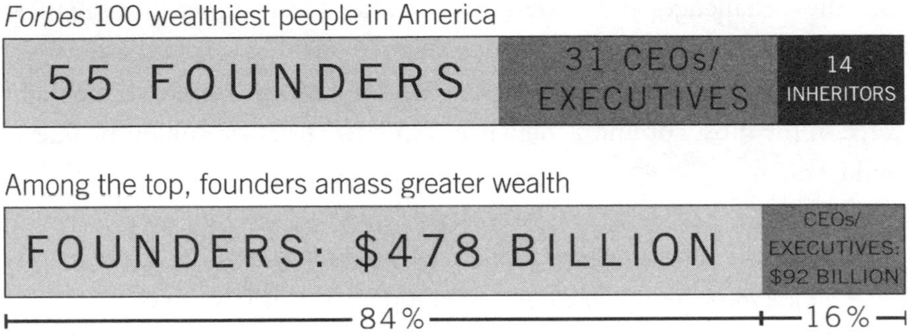

Musk, serial entrepreneur and owner of The Kitchen restaurant in Boulder, Colorado, "You don't follow someone's Smarts. You follow someone's Heart . . . [to] where they honestly and passionately want to go."[7]

Founders—Top Title and Top Reward

When asked, Silicon Valley entrepreneurs most often say *founder* is the title they covet the most. Not chairman, not CEO, but *founder*. In our own research we saw that over two-thirds of respondents prefer the founder title to all others. The market also disproportionately rewards the efforts of founders. A *Forbes* magazine analysis of the hundred wealthiest people in the United States (who have an astonishing aggregate net worth of $837 billion) uncovered three core sources of wealth: founders, CEOs, and inheritors.[8] Further parsing the list, we counted fifty-five founders, thirty-one CEOs, and fourteen inheritors. Of the roughly $570 billion that CEOs and founders control, founders represent an astonishing 84 percent. It turns out that not only is the founder title the most desirable, it is also the one the market rewards most (see figure 2-2).

The Limitations of Heart

If founders were the only reason and necessity for long-term business success, we could end the book here. But founders commonly reach a scale point where they need new capabilities, have to come face-to-face with trade-offs of Heart, and must consider the fundamental question of whether they really want to grow the business to the next level. We will discuss these challenges and trade-offs in chapter 4, but suffice it to say there are weaknesses to a Heart-driven approach to business. Like its sister traits of Smarts, Guts, and Luck, Heart has its limitations. Here, we highlight three of the most common challenges faced by Heart-dominant business-builders.

Limitation 1: Heart needs to be complemented by execution and market acceptance to become a business. Passion and ideas have to overlap with both innate capability and a hospitable market. Zeal, proficiency, and market create a potent intersection. If you lack the capability set or the market rejects your idea, Heart alone will not do the job. People may become impassioned by an idea. But will they be able to execute it? They may even spy a gap in the market, but is it really an attractive one? ("There is a gap in the market, but not a market in the gap," as a ZEFER cofounder and former HBS classmate of Tony's used to say.) In short, Heart's passion, capabilities, and market have to work in unison to create real—and magical—business potential (see figure 2-3).

Limitation 2: Heart can't just be about thinking big. While passion and storytelling are core capabilities required for Heart-dominant business-builders, founders need to translate that passionate narrative into a practical, legible plan of action. Over the years, we have encountered some very high-Heart, big-thinking people who could not communicate their idea simply, or were unwilling to propel their idea forward on a practical initial scale that allowed them to iterate and grow it over time. In some technological instances, an idea may be so ahead of its time that a business-builder has difficulty bringing it down a notch to make it generally understandable. "I don't care if people don't get it, I have clarity in my own head," is one potential weakness and limitation of the strong (read *stubborn*)-at-Heart. Relatedly, we've seen people who are eager to start something big, yet unwilling to prove it out first. At times, a Heart-dominant individual may believe that her idea itself is so big that nothing other than a think-big/start-big level will suffice. This is occasionally true, but it is the exception, not the norm. In terms of picking a realistic, practical, and smart starting

FIGURE 2-3

Passion, Capabilities, and Market Work in Unison

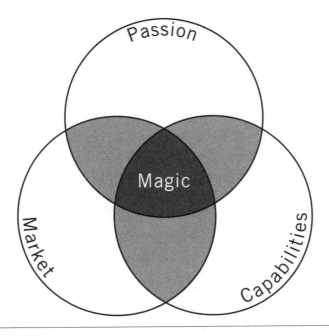

point, we live by the following principle: think big but be willing and open to starting small.

Limitation 3: A Heart-driven approach can yield diminishing returns. As we discuss further later, there are two inflection points in a business growth cycle where Heart has disproportionate impact and founders excel: at the conception period; and later at the rejuvenation, or extension, period, when the business needs to be reconfigured for new growth (which is why founders often launch a business, leave, and come back onboard: think Steve Jobs at Apple, or Howard Schultz at Starbucks). At the onset of business formation, a founder's and a business's personality are inextricably linked. Therein lie both the strength and weakness of the business. As businesses evolve toward a clear proof point and look to scale, they usually require more process, more delegation of responsibility, and often some trade-offs in the original vision for the sake of size. As we will discuss in chapter 7, here is where some of the limitations of Heart, and of founders

Do You Really Have Your Heart in Your Business?

Before business-builders take the leap of pursuing their ideas, we urge them to ask themselves the following Heart-related questions. These True North queries focus on the Heart, and are intended to discern, define, and refine a business-builder's vision and purpose. (There's a whole section of True North question sets in chapter 8.)

What is the purpose of your business, stated simply and clearly?

The right starting point for a business is to consider the *why* before the *what* and the *how*. Ask yourself if your business aligns with something you care about internally, that elicits a natural fire-in-the-belly passion and therefore is something that you can instinctively describe in the most simple of ways. The purpose of Starbucks as not just a coffee shop but a "third place" instantly resonates because it is just that—a third place in addition to work and home—for millions. Or consider the explosive growth of Uniqlo, the fast-fashion Japanese retailer, whose purpose is "making good casual clothes for all to wear." Your purpose statement should be straightforward as these and something that resonates with both you and your customer.

What is the (right-brained) essence of your business model?

The business world veers naturally toward left-brained, or rational, thinking. Yet roughly 90 percent of our decisions and our preferences are emotional (only afterward do we justify them based on their practicality or functionality). Since Heart-driven businesses are easy to feel, ask yourself: what are the emotional components of your business that will excite or engage a potential investor or consumer? Another way to think of this question is to reflect on what the romance of your product or service might be. This concept was captured brilliantly by a line in the documentary *The Pixar Story*: one of the studio's directors describes its business as understanding "how to make people feel."[9]

What are the *must-have* values of your business?

Just as plants need nutrients to grow, businesses need values to thrive. For Zappos founder Tony Hsieh, it came down to ensuring that his employees have bought into the Zappos ethos of "delivering happiness." Zappos offers new hires $2,000 to quit after the first week. Explains Hsieh, "The original motivation for doing it was to make sure that people were there for reasons beyond a short-term paycheck." But the biggest benefit of Zappos' "employee rebate" has been its impact on the employees who turn it down. Explains Hsieh, "They have to go home and think it over, and ask, 'Is this a company I can really commit to? Is it a company I believe in for the long-term?' When they come back to work on Monday, deciding to stay, they are that much more committed and passionate about the company and its values." Values represent the core principles that support your overall purpose.

What are you prepared to do when those values are violated? Or are there values you are willing to trade off for scale?

Economic pressures or changes in the financial climate can often force a company to breach its core principles. What trade-offs are you willing and unwilling to make against your company's values? This question often comes into play when companies need to scale up, raise funds, or consider tough leadership changes. As an example, we sometimes see a business that has affianced itself to "the wrong money"—a funding source whose values are a poor fit with a business's passion or purpose. In this scenario, will you look elsewhere to find another firm that allows you to sustain your core values? To what parts and values of your Heart must you remain uncompromisingly true? Understanding how strongly committed you are to your values, and what you are willing to do when those values are violated, is key.

What are the top five to eight nuances in your business that differentiate it from the rest?

As we have discussed, nuance represents one of the three defining elements of Heart. Consider the more subtle aspects of your differentiation that few would be able to discern if they were separated but as a collective create part of the magic that makes what you have unique.

The ultimate True North question on Heart: If you had all the money you could ever want, what would you be doing to occupy your life meaningfully?

Consider what it is that you care so much about that you must build a business around it. Many great businesses start out at a place where the lines between work and hobby intersect, overlap, and complement each other. As Confucius wrote, "The supreme accomplishment is to blur the line between work and play . . . and you will never have to work a day in your life."

To reframe the above: Are you doing what you're doing out of love, and the desire to make a difference—or are you in it for the money? *Both* is what too many people answer, but every now and then one is lucky enough to encounter the business equivalent of an artistic compulsion to bring to life a truly Heart-driven vision.

in general, come into play and other traits, such as Smarts, are required in higher proportion. A founder's natural desire or need to control even the smallest element of the company, or to maintain her perfectionist's vision, can restrict the scale and effectiveness of her idea. She must eventually decide: *what's more important—the idea or its reach?*

Recapping the Role of Heart in Business

Some years ago, a short clip of Kevin Spacey from the television series *Inside the Actors Studio* went viral. Speaking to host James Lipton, the actor said, "There is no prize out there. The only prize is this one—what you feel and what you accomplish. To be ambitious and to want to be successful is not enough. That is just desire. To know what you want, to understand why you are doing it, to dedicate every breath in your body to achieve—if you feel you have something to give, if you feel that your particular talent is worth developing and is worth caring for, then there is nothing you can't achieve."[10]

It is perhaps one of the best summaries that we have seen of the meaning of Heart.

Whether you are an artisan seeking to perfect a craft, a musician working toward capturing every note's nuance, an athlete dedicated to an intense daily training regimen, a founding team member building a business from the ground up, or an executive leader engaged in corporate business-building, unless you inject and impose a higher sense of purpose, your efforts will lack soul and be less likely to succeed. Purpose and passion are the foundations of Heart, and in some respects, the foundation of a business.

With purpose, Heart is persevering and passionate; it gives out and back to the world. To have purpose means giving individuals a product or service that is worth caring for and that has a clear *why*, or reason for being. As we have said, purpose need not be overly lofty or social, but should instead focus on being clear and reflective of underlying values. And while money will often flow to a business that delivers on its purpose, the purpose has to be something other than "making money." Examples of some of the purpose-driven questions we like are: *How might this make for happier consumers? More engaged learners? Smarter diets? Better decision making?*

"What we should worry about day after day is to provide quality products on time, within budget, to our customers," Narayana Murthy says he tells his colleagues at Infosys. "We must show transparency to investors, not violate any law of the land, and be in harmony with society. That's our main charter, and we should stick to it. The stock market may or may not reward us even if we do that. This is ephemeral. We should not be too ecstatic about it today or get despondent if it falls tomorrow."[11]

Core values are underused tools. They are the principles behind any purpose. They are the deep-rooted principles underpinning Heart—and the sum of why and how a business operates. Establish them collectively and authentically, and make them something you can commit to. Tony Hsieh says he initially "kind of resisted the idea" of defining his company's core values "because it seemed like one of those big corporate things to do. For us, the difference is that we wanted to come up with committable core values, meaning we're actually willing to hire and fire people based on them, regardless of, or independent of, their specific job performance."

For Apple, the values of design and experience are fundamentally integrated into everything the company does; for a company like Patagonia, purpose is about sustainability and having double bottom-line objectives; and for Steve Ells of the restaurant chain Chipotle, it is as much about trying to create more positive eating habits as it is about convenient food service.[12] These company examples and their values underpin the *purpose* of Heart (Heart's first defining element) and why it is worth *sacrificing* for (Heart's second element), and also why in the quest toward reaching the highest levels of that purpose and vision you need to increase levels of *nuance* (Heart's third element) that only those closely connected with the business can truly appreciate.

We can ultimately define, measure, and distill the meaning of Heart by recommending that entrepreneurs and business-builders ask themselves a basic question: *Does this idea, decision, or initiative "feel" right?* In the first stages, entrepreneurs rarely possess the luxury of having all the facts at hand. Nor do they (or anyone for that matter) possess the ability to see into the future.

To trust what you are feeling, to know it makes up the real Heart of you and your business, you need an unbreakable connection and consistency between what you do and your underlying principles and values. Ask yourself, how strong is the linkage between your behavior and your values? Doing what we say and saying what we do, and basing both on our principles and beliefs, creates a confidence and trust that is the greatest leverage for improved leadership, impact, and business-building potential.

In the venture capital business, we get a vicarious thrill out of witnessing the joy and passion of founders and their young companies that are out to change the world. By their very nature, these start-ups have a far better shot at creating and cultivating a special working environment. Founders tend to have the closest connection and consistency between a personal value set and a business behavior set because, ideally, that connection is the very reason they started something in the first place. Scaling culture—or more precisely, preserving your special culture as you grow—can be challenging. At some point in a firm's evolution, the emphasis on *big* can overtake, and play havoc with, a company's original purpose, values, and founding principles. Herein lies the challenge for Heart-driven leaders—to find a way to keep their fundamental values and purpose while understanding what trade-offs might be acceptable in the course of scaling.

This is where the other traits—Smarts, Guts, and Luck—come in. Achieving the right balance at critical stages of a company's growth and evolution is what presents business-builders with the greatest challenge. What is true at each stage and growth inflection point is that the Heart gels a company's purpose and drives long-term intrinsic motivation for employees. Steve Papa, the founder and CEO of Endeca, puts it well when he says simply, "Heart is the glue that keeps things going."[13] This Heart must be present as the foundational base of a firm. Most large businesses fall prey to overprocessing, overcodifying, and over-PowerPointing their story, strategy, and even culture. Herein lies the difference between genuine employee-centric, Heart-driven, soulful cultures and mediocre me-too businesses.

Don't believe us? Drop by any Container Store or Trader Joe's, or visit Zappos' headquarters in Las Vegas. You can't help feeling that the employees there are just plain happier. Ask them why. The answer is simple: they believe in the company's purpose, truly love its products and its service, and appreciate that the company understands their professional goals. They collectively share in the expression of the company's Heart.

There is a thin line between cult and culture. After all, every organization has its own culture. But few have a fervor, or an intense belief in their own purpose, that infuses everything they do. And that differentiates them from the rest of the crowd. Businesses that can create a soulful cultural movement among their employees are rare, yet those who can have a remarkable advantage they should celebrate and preserve.

If you watched one hundred Hollywood films in a row, you would be left with a recurrent theme: *Follow your heart.* Little wonder Heart has become more or less synonymous with fuzzy goal-seeking and perceived to be absent of rigor or critical intelligence. But from our perspective, Heart is anything but indistinct. Its three identifiable and defining characteristics— purpose with passion, sacrifice, and nuance—are unmistakable. In a skeptical era, many of us are wary of "believing" headlong in anything. Which is yet another reason why entrepreneurs and businesses with an authentic Heart have increased impact and why enormous courage, conviction, stamina, and hard work are required to express Heart fully.

Challenges and hard work are ahead of anyone wanting to create a company and build a meaningful business. The critical questions and litmus tests remain: if you could do anything you wanted because you already had all the money you wanted, what would you truly love to do? How would you change the world?

As always and against each of our entrepreneurial building traits of Heart, Smarts, Guts, and Luck, we emphasize the paramount importance of *self-awareness*, especially at the beginning stages of a new venture, and later on, when a person's effort or intensity bumps up against the churn of the business environment and at the various thresholds of business growth. But by casting aside fear and self-doubt to start and lead something with genuine vision and a clear Heart-driven purpose, you have taken the first step toward creating a lasting business.

CHAPTER IN SUMMARY

Heart: Winning with the Heart

- The Business Plan Myth: The starting point for a business is not a business plan. The starting point for a business is to look more internally, take time for self-reflection, and consider what one really cares to do and feels is worth doing, and from there to start by doing (rather than writing about doing). The start of the right trial or right sensible project (and subsequent ones) may be the most important input for the eventual business plan.

- The Components of Heart: Three defining elements: purpose and passion; sacrifice and *agape*, and nuance.

- Heart-Driven Entrepreneurs Start with Purpose and Passion: Heart-driven entrepreneurs are fueled by a sense of *purpose*, a calling toward a greater vision beyond a product or profit motive. Surrounding the purpose of any business is a set of core values or principles—they need not be stated, but they need to be *felt*. Establish core values collectively and authentically, and make them values that can be committed to.

- Sacrifices, Work Ethic, and *Agape*: The concept of *agape*, or sacrificial love, is a defining trait of Heart-driven entrepreneurs, especially founders. People are more than willing to shelve their personal comforts and needs to improve their business when they feel the cause is worth the care and sacrifice.

- Bringing on the Nuance: The *nuance* element of Heart is essential; it establishes authenticity by infusing a business with all of its subtleties, quirks, and imperfections. Much of what makes a business unique derives from the collective sum of the nuances that only the genuinely Heart-driven can provide.

- What Heart Isn't: Heart has nothing to do with *lust*, or with short-term intellectual romances. The Heart also cannot be defined by hard work alone. While sacrifice and *agape* represent the second defining element of Heart, hard work without passion is just that—hard work. The hard work of authentic Heart drives further commitment and intensity around the business purpose, while the hard work of something disconnected from purpose drives indifference and even resentment.

- Founders Are the Torchbearers of Heart: The founder is the most Heart-driven of our business-builder roles. More than any other, *Founder* is the most desired, and most rewarded, title.

- Pregnancy Envy and Rejuvenation: Heart flourishes and has its greatest impact during two stages: at the founding and at points of rejuvenated, *extension* growth. Founding refers to the start—the gestation, where a series of iterative "passion projects" help to shape the idea toward a first proof point. The extension period comes much later, when companies risk becoming victims of their own success. New competition and innovations require nearly all businesses to go through a rebirth point, requiring the founder-like skills once again.

- When Heart Fails: There are three key limitations of Heart. The first is the need for Heart's desire and passion to overlap with capability and an accepting market, the second is in translating a think-big vision into a start-small plan, and the third comes at the crossover between proof-of-concept and scale-up, where Heart-dominance may have diminishing returns.

- Making Magic Happen: The perfect intersection of Heart, capabilities, and market acceptance.

- Ultimate Test and True North Questions for Heart: Begins with a reflection on one's values, and mapping those values against what one would be doing if money and acclaim were not an objective. Starting with purpose and passion is the strongest leverage point for creating a lasting great business.

3
Smarts:
IQ IS ONLY THE BEGINNING

"Some people are just better." It's one of our favorite sayings. It follows, too, that some folks are just, well, *smarter* than others. Does it matter? Of course: having a baseline of Smarts is an essential foundation for any career path. And if you possess that rare intelligence where you are truly among the very best (commonly dubbed *genius*), well, you will probably do well in any professional path.

But for most entrepreneurs and business-builders, a baseline level of Smarts suffices. Trust us when we say you do not need to be a genius to be a great business-builder. Chances are you already have the necessary IQ threshold, and that you also possess some mix of the different *types* of Smarts to enhance your success potential. It is the capacity to use these different types of Smarts toward (as we will discuss) *pattern recognition* that is key.

Get Smart

The standard measure of Smarts is what we call *Book Smarts*, which reflect analytical prowess and intellectual discipline. The other types of Smarts are *Street Smarts*, *People Smarts*, and *Creative Smarts*. Without them, Book Smarts alone may lead you to technically great ideas that lack application or consumer appeal. Or worse, the ideas may be commercially attractive, but the overly Book Smarts individual may feel that she can or must do it all on her own.

Mix Book, Street, People, and Creative Smarts together, though, and you get the acumen, sensibility, and responsiveness we refer to as *Business Smarts*. The ultimate litmus test of Smarts lies in knowing how to temper and balance these four variants as you move from one decision to the next; for example, deemphasizing Book Smarts when a situation requires a more Street Smarts approach, or dialing up People Smarts when analysis alone might not provide a practical answer.

Cutting across each one of our Smarts categories and linking them together is your ability to connect the dots and recognize patterns. The term *pattern recognition* generally describes the way babies learn, but in this chapter and throughout this book we use it to refer to how adults achieve peak performance and mesh more successfully with the world. It turns out that the way babies hear via patterns is similar to how the best business thinkers and leaders learn and do. Indeed, we should reach back to think more like we did as infants! People gifted with the ability to recognize patterns are able to grasp macro and micro trends earlier and easily; they can see both straight ahead and "around the corner." Pattern recognition is at the very core of defining Business Smarts—an ability to recognize themes and patterns across the spectrum of Book, Street, Creative, and People Smarts.

In his 2009 book *The Wayfinders: Why Ancient Wisdom Matters in the Modern World*, anthropologist Wade Davis discusses the ability of ancient Polynesians to navigate for thousands of miles across the Pacific Ocean with no compass or other modern-day instrumentation. How did they do this? They evolved an incredible contextual intelligence that looked for associations between changes in the weather, water, and the ocean life around them: "They picked up on slight variations of cloud formation, the various tones of the sky, the number of stars they could see in the outer halo of high clouds, the way the dolphins swim toward sheltered waters as a storm is coming on, the salinity and taste of the water," summarized journalist David Brooks in the *New Yorker*. "In other words, they used slight perceptions, some conscious, some unconscious, to develop astounding maps of reality."[1] This pattern recognition capability remains what we feel to be the core of Smarts in today's business world.

Business Smarts Defined

Business Smarts \biz-nəs, -nəz smärts, ərts\ *noun* 1 : pattern recognition across Book Smarts, Street Smarts, People Smarts, and Creative Smarts, esp. in entrepreneurship

Pattern Recognition

$$\underbrace{}$$

Book Smarts + *Street Smarts* + *People Smarts* + *Creative Smarts*

Jack Hidary, the founder of job-search site Dice.com, defines this innate skill as the ability to "recognize patterns of success over time."[2] In turn, your ability to absorb and classify patterns generally leads to the creation and application of practical, repeatable habits that in time become automatic. Obviously, we value pattern recognition very highly. You can be off-the-charts-smart in any one of our four categories, but if you cannot swiftly identify, distill, and frame patterns across different types of Smarts, your insights will generally be compromised. In the pages ahead we will be re-capping the best *Smarts Habits* gleaned from some of the world's most successful entrepreneurs, as well as from our own experience, to show how each of our four categories of Smarts apply directly to business-building. Below, we take in order the four different types of Smarts that we see as critical components of entrepreneurial and business-building success. Ultimately, we will see how these categories come together to create Business Smarts.

Book Smarts

For most people, the word *smarts* connotes classic Book Smarts. Whether we're talking about a comfort with numbers, a capacity to decipher trends, or the ability to drill down around customer data, almost all good business-builders have some innate or acquired baseline analytical ability that leads to informed, objective, better managerial decision making.

Interestingly, in our HSGL survey research, Smarts, and especially as it relates to Book Smarts, often scored lower in relative importance to the other business-building traits of Heart, Guts, and Luck. It appears that business-building requires a baseline—that is, some *absolute* level—of brainpower, but once you are at that baseline, you'll have as much potential for business-building success as anyone else. Indeed, Smarts appears to be a requirement throughout all business-building cycles, but it alone cannot ever guarantee success.

If we look at the number of exceptionally high-IQ folks who end up in places like Harvard Business School, McKinsey & Company, or Goldman Sachs (to name just a few gold-plated brands), it becomes clear that Book Smarts does have some correlation with business success. All these institutions screen for a high level of Book Smarts. And the people who make it past that screen are given privileged access to professors, alumni, recruiters, and colleagues that puts them in an ecosystem that increases their probability for success.

It may come as no surprise, then, that a 2010 *U.S. News & World Report* survey showed that Ivy League and other top schools are disproportionately represented on CEO résumés. This survey found that *Fortune* 500 CEOs cumulatively received ninety-nine degrees from Harvard, Columbia, and the University of Pennsylvania. Some large state schools, including Ohio State and the University of Michigan, ranked very high as well. (As an additional point of interest, the University of Wisconsin ranked ahead of Stanford.) On the other hand, only about one in three *Fortune* 500 CEOs has an MBA. Nineteen have no college degree at all.

So Book Smarts can get you in the door and help solve many basic analytical issues. But after that, its importance often wanes. During companies' ideation, launch, and start-up phases, Book Smarts can sometimes be as much an impediment as a boon. As venture capitalists, we have seen our share of pitches and have participated as judges in several business-plan competitions. What is amazing is how many times we see people overthink, overresearch, and overanalyze. (And this statement comes from a group that is pretty analytical.) It is not whether you should be analytical, but rather when, and what analysis can help you achieve. There are some things that are best "researched" by simply doing them and others by thinking and analyzing primary and secondary sources. In the mid-1990s, our coauthor Tony was in business school, and it was pretty clear to most that there was something important happening with the Internet. Over the next few years, many people tried to analyze and predict what would happen. Several business plans were developed as part of field study research projects and business-plan competitions, but by Tony's estimate, at best a single-digit percentage of those actually materialized into businesses. For many, so much time was spent poring over market sizing, projections, competitive landscapes, and other classic business-plan analyses that would-be entrepreneurs either convinced themselves out of the opportunity (with "precisely incorrect" rather than "approximately correct" information) or they missed a window of great opportunity.

Across our research, it was in the scale-up and later growth and mature stages of a company's life cycle that we found the most evident correlations between Book Smarts and executive success. Sometimes at these inflection points a new business plan is required. At other times it is about understanding which trade-offs to make in order to scale up the business.

The clearest examples of Book Smarts involve simplifying the complex with logic. Economist Esther Duflo and her colleagues at MIT's Abdul Latif Jameel Poverty Action Lab have focused on rethinking global poverty through the scientific method and randomized trials. In a 2010 TED talk, Duflo described how she tried to resolve an important policy debate over how best to encourage the use of mosquito bed nets to help stop the spread of malaria. She started by breaking the issue down into three straightforward questions:

- If people must pay for bed nets, will they buy them?

- When people get bed nets for free, will they use them?

- Do free nets discourage future purchases?

Rather than being ideological about these questions, Duflo looked for empirical tests that would answer them. She ran an experiment in Kenya giving people vouchers (at various discount levels) for bed nets, to compare with people buying them outright. Unsurprisingly, there was a direct inverse relationship between effective price and willingness to purchase the bed net. Further, those who got bed nets for free were no less likely to use them than those who purchased them. Finally, those who were given a free bed net were *more* likely than those who purchased one for $1–$3 to buy a bed net one year later at a $2 price point. Handing out bed nets does not discourage future purchases—it encourages them. An intensely debated policy question was answered by looking at the right questions and right measurement methods through a simple experiment. That's Smarts.

Similarly, many Web-based start-ups use this kind of "A/B" testing of different product features or different user experiences to see what works best with end-users. This new-product-development philosophy of agile or iterative development has its foundation in the same scientific method as Duflo's mosquito net experiments.

To review, here's what we've observed about Book Smarts:

1. High levels of Book Smarts may matter more for business scaling in larger organizations than in earlier stage start-ups.

2. Entrepreneurs and business-builders require some baseline of Book Smarts, but that baseline is probably not as high as they think. The critical component is really a set of Book Smarts *habits* that we describe below.

3. Top-of-the-line SAT and GMAT scores and degrees from top universities are merely one vector of Smarts. Other varieties of Smarts will always come into play.

The ability to organize, simplify, and prioritize is perhaps the most important quality we see in Smarts-oriented individuals. In contrast, the Heart-dominant person tends to make decisions based on passion and intuition (in a more organic pattern), and the Guts-dominant individual may make it a point to drive forward inexorably ("checklist manager" style) with less regard to the priority. Both could learn from the Smarts-dominant business-builder.

We highly endorse the following three Book Smarts habits (highlighted in the boxes below) that we have seen Book Smarts leaders use to their advantage. Two are about disciplined processes: writing an annual memo to the board, and creating a framework for better, shorter meetings. The other, using the right set of input versus output metrics, involves being smarter about analysis.

Smartest Book Smarts Habit #1

Write an Annual CEO Memo to the Board

At year-end, we sit down with each of our portfolio company CEOs. We ask them to list their top priorities for the upcoming year, as well as the lessons they've learned over the past twelve months: What patterns did they see in their business? What did they decide to do with those lessons?

We carry out this exercise in the form of a CEO memo to the board. It may sound simple, but it clarifies the big picture and creates a powerful mechanism for alignment between boards and CEOs. It is also one of the best focusing tools we know. In some way, shape, or form, the best business-builders we have met are highly disciplined in putting down their top priorities at a regular cadence.

The bottom line? Writing stuff down clarifies thoughts. And regularly revisiting and circulating those thoughts drives alignment. Here is our five-point plan on how entrepreneurs and business-builders should consider developing and using a CEO memo to the board:

1. At year's end, CEOs should prepare an annual memo articulating the five most important priorities for the upcoming twelve months. A new priority cannot be added until one is completed. Too many would-be entrepreneurs and business-builders fail because of "shiny ball syndrome"—something new catches their eye before an existing priority is completed.

2. Of these five priorities, the first should almost always be: "Achieve the financial plan." The memo should refer to the top-line and bottom-line targets, or to the date when management and board will agree on these targets. Compensation plans should align to these financial targets.

3. Additional priorities beyond achieving the financial plan reflect the top strategic initiatives for the year, which may include new product launches, customer service enhancements, or new market locations.

4. We then use this memo as a recurring framework for update discussions and board meetings. For example, throughout the year, the

first page of each board meeting presentation often reiterates and updates the major priorities set down in the annual memo. The memo's priority agenda serves to remind all board and management members what is most important and also gives us an opportunity to drill deeper into any one of the specific priorities.

5. Articulating lessons learned is crucial, too. We can accept failure, but we cannot accept not learning from past mistakes. Once a year, a CEO should share with the board and with employees the most important lessons she learned over the past twelve months, and what they mean for the organization going forward.

We know that most CEOs feel that they already carry out some version of this exercise, but rarely do we see it done simply and consistently. Do they really write out priorities and lessons so that it becomes an annual touchstone document? Throughout the year, it should become a *Groundhog Day* agenda guide to measuring progress against the big picture. Before every board meeting, this copy of a CEO memo to the board should reappear as a "level set" and reminder mechanism. It is one of the few process rules we wholeheartedly embrace.

Smartest Book Smarts Habit #2

Use Dashboards, but Focus on the Inputs, Not the Outputs

If priority setting with a CEO memo is the first Book Smarts habit, the second is to regularly consult a dashboard of performance indicators. This dashboard should include both leading and lagging indicators, and it should emphasize inputs over outputs.

Smarts-dominant entrepreneurs are often obsessed with numbers, results, and metrics (authors' admission: sometimes we are, too!). That's fine, but many business-builders confess to us that they spend too much time focusing on financial performance targets rather than on the inputs that drive those numbers. They go straight to the results without understanding what caused them. Why? Because boards, investors, and management demand objective performance measures.

Financial performance, though, is inevitably a by-product and consequence of something else. Financial numbers serve as a valuable scorecard, but they do not help us understand how to score, or even *why* we score. Ask a team to chase after results, and you may never be certain what drove those results, even if they turn out to be successful. And by the time you look at a financial result, it is usually too late to do anything about it. If you peruse both the results and the operating metrics that drive performance, you have a chance of influencing the results early on.

Pick your term: *operating metrics, leading indicators, customer metrics.* These inputs correlate to, or drive, the desired results of a business. If you focus on the inputs that appeal to customers—including the *whys* of customer satisfaction, convenience, or product quality—you can advance to the next *why*, which measures customer retention, or customer referral rate (Net Promoter Score, for example). Ultimately you will find you worry less about the final financial outputs.

Two concrete examples will shed additional light. In many of our retail or restaurant, investments, we espouse a value proposition of *convenience*. The more convenient we can make the consumer experience, the happier the customer will be. For example, one of our Cue Ball portfolio companies, MiniLuxe, is focused on being "the Starbucks of nail salons." Its weekly dashboard measures "turn-aways" (when prospective customers can't get appointments)—an unfulfilled promise of convenience. The goal is to delight customers so they return. The more likely customers are to return, the more apt they are to refer the experience to others— which translates not only into higher revenues, but a higher *quality* of revenues.

As a proxy for convenience, we measure things like turn-away rates and service wait times. *Convenience* means keeping those numbers as low as possible. If we detect the possibility of a chronic issue, we figure out how to solve it, perhaps through improved reservations systems or hiring additional staff. Other metrics include weekly cleanliness scores, customer loyalty, and periodic customer satisfaction reviews. We consider these operating metrics alongside financial results, but our goal is always to uncover the correlation between operating drivers and financial outcomes.

Businesses need to focus on the three to five metrics that represent the most crucial drivers of value creation. Focusing on these metrics will align an organization toward doing the right thing in a repeatable, scalable way. A weekly or monthly dashboard that highlights not just the financial results but also the operating metrics is smart, sensible, and actionable. This dashboard should be an exception-based report, allowing you to hunt down deviations from the norm.

Typically, people base their behavior on how their performance is measured. Below are a few guidelines on how to create a culture driven by operating metrics that focus on the right stuff:

1. Ensure that management understands the difference between leading indicators (operating metrics) and lagging indicators (financial results). The latter are for number-crunching analysts. The former are for managers and automatically lead to financial metrics.

2. Clearly communicate the most important operating metrics across the organization. It takes some thought to filter through the many possible options. Pick only the three to five operating metrics that correlate most highly to your desired financial goals and get people focused on those.

3. Regularly review an operating metric dashboard and focus on exceptions. Use a simple flash report or dashboard that encompasses the customer and operating metric inputs you share with your people, and you'll be able to scan the health of your business quickly. The goal is to focus on the exceptions—that is, where you are falling out of hand. A metric dashboard is akin to a set of regular blood tests or medical vitals results. It matters less where you fall into the normal range, and more where your tests or vitals are out of hand or "at risk."

Smartest Book Smarts Habit #3

Don't Waste Another Minute: Run Better, Shorter Meetings

Outside of general relationship building, we know of only three functional purposes for having a business meeting:

- To inform and bring people up to speed

- To seek input from people

- To ask for approval

Use the above as a filter to determine why you are having a meeting, then explain that purpose to your audience. Gatherings will often cut across multiple objectives, but forcing yourself to clarify the agenda into these three purposes will result in more effective, less wasteful meetings.

Consider a meeting that sets its agenda goals along the lines of: "I want to bring you up to speed on these two things"; "I need input on this item"; and "I would like to seek your approval on these outstanding issues." Yup, that's it—a simple three-purpose meeting rule that frames the goals of the meeting from the perspective of the meeting participant.

It's one of our business mantras: *Our strengths are our weaknesses and our weaknesses are our strengths.* With her innate preoccupation with focused priorities and metrics-driven analytics, the Book Smarts individual has a powerful edge over peers who are challenged with prioritization, analysis, and process. Yet that very same attentiveness can also work against her. She must understand the big picture inspiration and vision and at times step back from all the data and inputs by making a judgment or gut call about what needs to change. In short, sometimes inspiration and judgment can capture the wide-angle vista that the close-up snapshot of analytics misses.

We have seen people with extremely high levels of Book Smarts who get so enmeshed in numbers, charts, and diagrams that they ignore the practical solution staring them in the face. The result? "Paralysis by analysis," or as

Dick likes to say, "You don't always need to count the ant's eyebrows." Any action is better than inaction. Once they take action, overly Book Smarts people may find themselves critically second-guessing information that is still taking shape around them. They forget to "Just Nike It."

In their quest to be right and to root out answers, super–Book Smarts people can be their own worst enemies. The three authors enjoy recalling a meeting they took with legal counsel to analyze the complex tax consequences of a particular transaction. After spending long hours with the lawyers trying to determine the impact of each scenario and how to best draft the legal documents to optimize tax efficiency, one of our colleagues asked about the likely tax bill relative to the potential savings of being "smarter" about the tax solution. Turns out that the legal work required to make the transaction more tax efficient cost more than the prospective tax savings! We were all lost in a moment of being overly Book Smart. As with all things, balance is key.

This is where Street Smarts can come into play.

Street Smarts

Street Smarts is a trait we typically associate with someone who has risen to success through experience, tenacity, and a few skinned knees. More often than not, lacking formal education, she learns from real-life experience and vanquishes any obstacles in her way to ultimate career success. The Street Smarts business-builder is the ultimate business anthropologist—observing events and people around her, and taking in and processing her observations and experiences. CEOs like Jim Skinner of McDonald's or Brian Dunn of Best Buy cut their teeth early in modest positions. Skinner served as a restaurant manager, and Dunn worked as a store associate. The mailroom-to-boardroom career trajectory may take place less often than it used to, but no amount of Book Smarts can replace the intuition and practical wisdom that come from real-life education and experience.

Vital to the growth of any business, Street Smarts individuals bring a hardheaded practicality and momentum that cuts through stasis. They read situations and contexts rather than statistics. They rely on observation, experience, and common sense to come up with what seems to be an obvious solution that their Book Smarts colleagues may never have considered. The successful Street Smarts individual has an unnerving pragmatism about herself and can be anyone from a scrappy underdog to someone who is systematically pragmatic in her decision making. But she brings to the table a highly tuned sense-and-respond capability that adapts to the environment as necessary.

Experience—and pragmatically driven Street Smarts—serve as a necessary complement to Book Smarts. Business school will teach you the theory and best practices of marketing and negotiation, but unless you've done them, learned from your mistakes, and moved forward, you will lack the practical, intuitive grasp of how they work. We have long believed that business schools should spend more time instilling in students the practical skills of selling and communicating. Reading countless case studies cannot substitute for the Street Smarts gained by spending a year on the road selling door-to-door.

Sometimes Street Smarts can yield solutions to even the toughest problems, often because others just overlook the simple ideas. Or constraints can force you to be creative and pragmatic. Dr. Vilayanur S. Ramachandran, a leading neuroscientist and head of the Center for Brain and Cognition at the University of California, San Diego, is known for his simple, low-tech experiments in a field ruled by million-dollar imaging machines. Take, for example, chronic phantom limb pain, in which a patient feels pain or cramping in a limb that has been amputated. In place of expensive therapy sessions or lab imaging visits—treatments range from electrical nerve stimulation, to further surgery (removing scar tissue near nerves), to medications such as antidepressants—Dr. Ramachandran's solution was a $5 household mirror. He sets up a mirror where the missing limb would be and arranges the patient's opposite, real limb so that the patient sees the mirror (and in it, the reflection of the real limb) where the phantom one should be. Telling the patient to move both limbs together, in the same motion, and seeing in the mirror the reflection of the real one (but what effectively appears to be the phantom one moving) has actually relieved patients of this terrifying and "imagined" pain.

In the venture capital industry, we often encourage our colleagues to gain hands-on operating experience. Having operating experience often helps make you a better venture capitalist, but becoming a VC does not necessarily make you a better operator. Consider our Cue Ball partner,

Smartest Street Smarts Habit #1

Use the Three-Minute Rule

The Street Smart entrepreneur is a business anthropologist. We ask CEOs of our portfolio companies to dive deep—really deep—to learn about every conceivable dimension of their customers. This means carrying out customer-driven research that goes beyond the traditional tools such as cluster and conjoint analysis to uncover what different customers want most. Many of the most interesting insights and patterns have to do with the larger context within which a product or service is being used. Thankfully, there are some Street Smarts tools to help those with less natural ethnographic capability.

We believe the three-minute rule is the best such tool. It is based on a simple premise: you can learn a great deal about customers by finding out what they are doing three minutes immediately *before* and three minutes *after* they use your product or service. Context matters. Among the products at Thomson was one that provided investment analysts with financial earnings data. Until Dick Harrington and Tony Tjan applied the three-minute rule, we hadn't fully appreciated that shortly after they received our data, many analysts painstakingly imported and reformatted the data into Excel. This observation led us to develop a more seamless Excel plug-in feature with enhanced formatting capability. The result was a significant and almost instantaneous uplift in sales.

The three-minute rule also helps spotlight nonintuitive selling opportunities. In one retail-customer research assignment during Tony's consulting days, he noticed that new mothers commonly purchased both diapers and digital cameras. Observing how people shopped in stores revealed that new moms who purchased diapers were more likely to be interested in digital camera accessories (presumably to capture the memories of their diapered little ones). Placing these two seemingly unalike product categories closer together stimulated greater cross-selling. You need to follow customers' shopping patterns or look over their shoulder while they use your product to understand what might otherwise be a missed improvement opportunity.

Our friend, shopping anthropologist Paco Underhill, has filmed hundreds of thousands of hours of consumer behavior in retail settings in the United States and overseas. In his book *Why We Buy*, he describes how customers buy less when their arms are full, as they're busy making their way to the checkout counter. Underhill concluded that managers should consider placing shopping baskets in the middle of the store to keep customers in shopping mode longer, since once inside the store, few customers bother to return to the entrance to fetch a basket.[4]

It's easy, isn't it, to fall prey to conventional patterns? The three-minute rule is a tool to recognize new patterns. At Thomson, for example, we saw ourselves as a data provider. In fact, we were really part of a broader workflow solution that included other software, in that case Microsoft's Excel. In the cross-selling of diapers with cameras and Underhill's shopping-basket examples, the three-minute rule reminds us of the advantages of rechoreographing the context of a shopping experience to better meet customer patterns.

Customers are in search of solutions. The three-minute rule obliges all of us to see the context in which a customer is using our products, and therefore also the bigger picture, with all its adjacent opportunities.

Smartest Street Smarts Habit #2

Appreciate the Power of Pause

Dick Harrington's uncle has a saying: "Play stupid and win smart." Not surprisingly, this uncle is a great poker player gifted with uncanny emotional restraint.

We believe this playing-stupid-to-win-smart philosophy has applications well beyond poker. In general, our human impulse is to speak our minds. That is, talk first, then think and act later. It's far better to pause and think before speaking.

Many entrepreneurs are natural extroverts who may find it difficult to appreciate this strategy. Yet pausing before reacting can make a significant difference in the outcome of a business negotiation. Consider this DVR-inspired approach to sensitive business situations:

1. **Pause.** Think of business situations as an ongoing mini-movie. You are the director. If filming is disrupted for any reason—new information becomes available; a competitive advantage appears; available resources change, etc.—your first call to action should be to . . . pause.

2. **Play.** Let the movie play out in your head. Now consider various scenarios in which you can use any or all disruptions to your advantage.

3. **Mute.** Remind yourself to hit your internal mute button. That way, you keep your thoughts private unless there is a compelling reason to blurt them out. Think like a poker player. Is there any upside to blurting out what you know with others? There usually isn't.

4. **Rewind and record again.** Appropriately reset your actions and hit "Record" again to move toward your desired win-smart ending.

The act of pausing to contemplate the various scenarios that are likely to unfold is critical. As in physics, every action has an equal and opposite reaction. The key here is to avoid unintended consequences.

Let's connect the pause, play, mute, rewind/record pattern using an example. In a recent negotiation to buy a company, it came to our attention that another party had placed an offer on the table. It turned out that the rival party was a consortium with whom we were planning to partner on the same deal. (We had proposed this opportunity to them shortly before the negotiation began.) Our knee-jerk instinct was to call them up, offer appropriately harsh criticism, and then inform them that we were through working with them.

Instead, we paused. How would taking that course of action benefit us? It wouldn't have. It would only have made us feel better at that moment, but do little else to advance us toward our bigger goal of closing the deal.

By carefully fast-forwarding the likely outcomes of this "movie," we landed on another approach. We would remain silent and use our knowledge to our advantage. Why? Let's take our three scenarios one by one:

- Scenario A: Get mad, with the result that our would-be partners have no opportunity to explain, and our reaction hindering the probability of ever working with them

- Scenario B: Get mad before locking in a range of alternative partners who might do the deal with us, which may mean no deal whatsoever

- Scenario C: Get mad and announce that we can do the deal our-selves, causing the other party to bid up the price on the deal and win it

By remaining silent, we effectively played stupid and won smart. Our knowledge gave us two pieces of invaluable insight. First, the other guys showed how much they really wanted to do the deal, and second, their attempts to get the deal exclusively showed a lack of professional proto-col and gave us an early warning signal that these were not partners with whom we wanted to work. In short order, we mobilized another partner on the deal and proposed a joint deal at the original agreed-on price, which the target company accepted.

In moments of high emotion, it is easy to forget our desired goal. In this case, it was to win the deal at a reasonable price. Our allies en route to winning smart? Silence and restraint.

John Hamel. Aggressive, opinionated, strong-willed, and at ease in his own skin, John is a great example of a Street Smart entrepreneur (overall, he personifies the Guts/Smarts profile). After growing up in a blue-collar town, John graduated from Harvard and spent several years as an entrepre-neur in technology and real estate. Recognizing that the medical and legal communities in his hometown ran their operations out of triple-decker houses, he built a professional office complex in the heart of town (on his weekends off, no less). In no time at all, he had a 100 percent occupancy rate. "Could I have done a study?" John speculates today, "or figured out how many doctors, dentists, and attorneys there were?"[3] He did neither.

Instead, based on his own instincts and Guts, he seized an opportunity before anyone else could.

John defines Street Smarts as a combination of instinct and the ability to connect with a wide spectrum of people from all backgrounds, professions, and income levels. It's about being practical, responsive, and respectful to your audience and your environment. Make no mistake, John also has Book Smarts, but he knows when to dial down an academic approach in favor of a more practical, instinctive, and even hardheaded one.

Some of the best Street Smarts business-builders we know are in effect skilled anthropologists. The Book Smarts individual may possess the capacity to amass and divide countless data points, but the Street Smart founder can adapt and grow her business simply by observing the environment in which she interacts with her clients or customers. This pragmatic feel allows the Street Smart business-builder to understand the notion of *context*. Among the most important anthropological lessons we have learned from street-savvy entrepreneurs is the *three-minute rule*, which involves understanding what your customer is doing three minutes before and three minutes after using your product. This rule is the first of a pair of Street Smarts Habits (highlighted in the boxes).

People Smarts

People Smarts is a close relative to Street Smarts, but it has its own distinct traits. Whether we are talking about businesses, brands, schools, or institutions, in the end it all comes down to people. When Thrillist founder and chief executive Ben Lerer bought the online shopping community JackThreads, what he was really buying, he says, was "a business partner [JackThreads founder and CEO Jason Ross] who is . . . a force of nature and somebody I wanted to be partners with." He adds, "At the end of the day, the way I've always done it is with a gut check."[5] Especially with people, "you feel it or you don't feel it. If you feel it, then you move fast. If you don't, you run away as quickly as you can."

While Lerer's People Smarts may sound purely instinctive, business-builders with good People Smarts possess three skills that *can* be honed: intuiting how people will react in particular situations, prioritizing relationships, and developing talent. The first means having a feel for how the constellation of potential interrelationships between people are likely to play out—a soothsayer ability to see things from the other side, as it were, before acting. The second is the ability to effectively prioritize and manage the relationships that are most important to success—not in a Machiavellian sense but rather in an intuitive, practical, unshameful manner. And finally, the third is the ability to attract, develop, and retain good people by zeroing in on what really motivates them. We'll be sharing a Smarts Habit on each of these skills shortly, but let's first describe them.

A People Smarts business-builder engages a pattern recognition that decodes and intuits how people will react. This responsive, intuitive skill gives her a significant advantage, as she can factor her perceptions of the opinions of others into her decision making. Her comprehension of others' intentions and actions helps her to create and maintain strong relationships and, by anticipating the next moves of her business rivals, maintain her competitive edge in the marketplace.

In their book *Make Your Own Luck*, authors Eileen Shapiro and Howard Stevenson chronicle Kimberly-Clark's decision to raise the price of its diapers, on the assumption that chief rival Procter & Gamble would quickly follow suit. Surprise: P&G did not increase its price, and by throwing in promotions and coupons, quickly began to dominate the marketplace. Had Thomas J. Falk, the CEO of Kimberly-Clark, considered how P&G's famously market share seeking CEO A.G. Lafley, might react, Falk would have likely pursued a different pricing strategy.[6]

Individuals with strong People Smarts are gifted with that ability to visualize how others will respond to and connect with one another. Stephen Schwarzman, CEO and cofounder of Blackstone, one of the world's largest and most successful investment firms, cites his ability to understand how other people think as a key factor in his success. As an undergraduate at Yale, the private equity titan-to-be didn't study economics or finance, but Culture and Behavior—a mixture of psychology, sociology, biology, and anthropology. Today, both as an investor and the builder of a firm, Schwarzman tries to "look at every situation from the perspective of every group and every person involved with it . . . to figure out if there's a way to satisfy everyone's needs, or predict what people will want to do."[7] From his perspective, it has worked out well because "you often can see changes coming in the world as the result of thinking about what is on the minds of everybody who's involved with the situation."

Beyond knowing the interplay between people, you have to know which set of folks might really drive your success. Just as it is critical to know your very top customers, it is key to know the small set of relationships that have the potential to really catapult your success. Keith Ferrazzi, former chief marketing officer of Deloitte Consulting and Starwood Hotels, is perhaps best known for his book *Never Eat Alone*. He is adamant in his belief that "a predictor of someone's success is the process by which they manage relationships."[8] The two key factors, Ferrazzi says, are a person's "capacity to accelerate relationships, and then to manage those relationships." Step one, according to Ferrazzi? "Every entrepreneur should be aware of the twenty-five people who are most important to the growth and success of your business. It is a critical, strategic question." Step two is the proactive, authentic cultivation of those relationships. But how do you get to your personal short list of top relationships?

Presumably, your top set of game-changing relationships would include people who would be part of a dream team for your business, a wish list from your "fantasy talent pool." One of the most important lessons we have gleaned through our own experiences and our interviews with entrepreneurs is that you always need to start your people pipeline much earlier than you think.

While People Smarts are inherently more feelings than frameworks, we want to share a few People Smarts Habits that can accelerate your awareness and acumen. The three Habits that follow—how to have critical conversations, how to cultivate a network, and how to motivate employees—can be implemented right away and have a big impact on your success. Additionally, we also provide a perspective on what to do when you are faced with the situation of having the wrong people on board (see "On the Firing Line" for one particular kind of dilemma).

On the Firing Line

It is a fact. Most small companies that start out fail, and this is frequently because their leaders had difficulty making the tough people decisions.

There is no doubt that firing can be very difficult, but you jeopardize the entire organization by keeping someone who is not qualified to do his job. And the firing process is also important for your own success, because if you are not tough enough to make the right decision, it may eventually cost you your own job. If you bring in a new person who is not as good as the old, or if you keep someone who is a drain on the company, then that says a lot about you as a leader and a decision maker. And the rest of the organization is certainly watching you to see whether you make the right moves.

In deciding who should be fired, it is best not to think about the organization in terms of people, but rather the roles or "hats" that need be donned and then find the individuals to fit them. This way of thinking can be especially useful when you are restructuring your company. As a role changes, redefine what it requires. Does the hat still fit the person currently wearing it? If not, you may have to place it on another head.

Finally, don't forget that the firing process can be a strong positive force in your company. No one who is giving her job 100 percent wants to glance to the side and see someone who is not working nearly as hard and yet is getting paid a comparable amount.—Dick Harrington

Smartest People Smarts Habit #1

Prepare for Critical Conversations

Because leaders can only accomplish things through others, the best leaders know how to have critical and courageous conversations. Not only do they know how to have these conversations, but they can anticipate the likely outcome of those conversations.

While we live in a technologically advanced and digitally intercon- nected world, the most important leadership conversations still take place in person. As far as staying connected and trading information are concerned, virtual communications such as e-mail, SMS, Twitter, and Facebook are faster, cheaper, and handier than the in-person alterna- tives. But problems arise when people use these tools to dodge critical or challenging messages that can significantly affect a business. Good leaders embrace technology that enhances communication productivity, but they also recognize the importance of in-person conversations when they need to address or accomplish difficult things.

Business-builders should learn to master three types of critical conver- sations: one-on-one meetings, small-group discussions, and one-to-many town-hall-style convenings. The success of each depends on the partici- pants, the setting, the credibility and thoroughness of your intent, and how you respond to, and engage with, your audience.

The Right Participants and the Appropriate Setting

In setting up a conversation, make sure you've invited the right people and chosen the right kind of meeting. Are you holding multiple one-on- ones when you should be interacting with a group (or vice versa)? Should you restrict attendance to certain senior members? Do you embrace—or avoid—town halls? Does the setting permit good eye contact? Does it convey an appropriate informality? If necessary, does it promote reflec- tive dialogue? Try out different formats, include (or exclude) one or two regulars, see what happens, and learn from it.

Credible and Complete Intent

Your audience should understand and believe the declared intent of the conversation. In preparing for your next one-on-one, list the outcomes you desire, kicking off with concrete ones such as, "She will agree to these two specific performance goals," and continuing until you've exhausted the more abstract ones, such as, "She knows that I really want her to succeed and will do everything I can to help her." A one-on-one chat can encompass up to a dozen desired outcomes.

Tsun-yan scored numerous one-on-one conversations held by Asian CEOs and CXOs by objectives and found a median score of only 43 percent of intended objectives met. During difficult conversations, even senior executives have trouble being either direct or comprehensive with their pre-meeting objectives. Moreover, they tend to miscommunicate abstract messages (e.g., "I want her to think I still believe in her potential") even more often than concrete messages (e.g., "You failed to deliver the second-quarter results"). We should add that these abstract messages are often the most important ones to get right! We encourage business-builders to prepare a complete list of intents and, depending on their ease with the more abstract ones, discuss ahead of time how best to convey them. Without carefully preconsidering your desired intent for a meeting, you will dramatically decrease your chances for a successful meeting.

Responsiveness and Emotional Engagement

By making a caring, emotional connection, the best leaders go beyond good listening. They sense and respond to others' needs as they come up, thereby building trust. While staying true to their values, good leaders are willing to adjust their goals during the conversation based on what they discover about others' needs. This does not mean they agree to whatever the other party wants, only that they remain open to a set of shared outcomes.

The capacity to engage in direct, persuasive, in-person conversations is an essential leadership skill. Executives seldom ask for help in finessing their conversation skills. They're far more likely to ask for help in improving teamwork at the top, creating greater empowerment down the line, catalyzing innovation, and helping better align board expectations. Investigate many of these familiar issues, and you'll usually find that the right conversations either never happened or failed to produce necessary outcomes. Companies and leaders quite simply can't afford this.

Smartest People Smarts Habit #2

Cultivate Your Network: Triage and Focus

Li Lu, the founder and chairman of Himalaya Capital Management, once shared a tip he learned from his close friend and mentor, Charlie Munger, vice chairman of Berkshire Hathaway. It boils down to the following rough mathematical equation: Out of every hundred people we meet, most of us can survive by never encountering fifteen of those people again. On the opposite end, we immediately feel a strong first-impression connection with five of those people. Focus on them. Although we will generally create some degree of a relationship with eighty of the one hundred people (one hundred people minus the fifteen we have "fired" immediately and the five we want to "hire" into our network), Li suggests we leave the "remaining middle" up to chance.

By focusing on the five out of one hundred, you are more likely to cultivate individuals who can genuinely affect your business success. Again, this is not to suggest you completely bypass the "fat middle" of your new relationships, only that you be more selective about how you spend your time. In today's Facebook and Twitter world, where it has become a badge of influence to boast enormous amounts of friends or followers, there is much to be said for filtering your circle of acquaintances to those who can make a difference for you.

In short, each time you find yourself at a large gathering or event, reflect afterward on the five people you should make efforts to stay in touch with. Leave the others up to chance.

Consider coupling this Munger "5 percent" rule with relationship guru Keith Ferrazzi's recommendation to constantly know and refresh the list of twenty-five people in this world who could take your business to the next level. These may be prospective customers, employees, or partners. The point is that by knowing and working on your relationship goals, you get an early indicator of success—the stronger your ability to build some of those twenty-five relationships, the stronger your future financial results are likely to be.

Smartest People Smarts Habit #3

Focus on the Intrinsic Reward as Much or More Than the Extrinsic

There is a very simple secret to attracting and creating long-term employee loyalty and retention (and no, it is not money, perks, or stock options). It is by giving your people meaningful roles.

This is not an idealistic mom-and-apple-pie dream, but rather a basic condition of human behavior and psychology that many businesses and leaders often forget: people are driven as much or more by intrinsic meaning as they are by extrinsic rewards.

Look around your social circle and you'll realize that some of your brightest friends work at places that pay jack-all relative to what they could be earning elsewhere. They are in those jobs because they provide fulfillment and a sense of purpose beyond the job.

In life, people make the "love or money" trade-off all the time. What can businesses do to minimize this trade-off? It comes down to balancing the intrinsic with the extrinsic rewards. The former is the heart and soul of an organization and a person's reason for working there. The latter is the practical mind and wallet. Here are four design points toward unlocking the secret of long-term employee loyalty:

1. **Help her create a meaningful role.** Ask in an interview what she would be doing if she had all the money she needed; explain and remind the employee why her role is critical and how it fits into the bigger picture. This is the foundation and most critical component of long-term retention.

2. **Give feedback.** Do so regularly, honestly, and thoughtfully.

3. **Offer professional development.** Keep her larger career path in mind; ask what she wants most to learn. People want to know where they are heading and that you care about helping them get there.

4. **Say thank you.** This means giving her both intrinsic and extrinsic recognition. Reaffirm your appreciation for her role (a simple hand-

written note or verbal thanks from time to time goes a long way), and pay her fairly.

Making people happy at their jobs is not as hard as it seems.

Creative Smarts

Our final category, Creative Smarts—which includes the ability to grasp patterns that others don't, and even lasso in new ones—is key to any true visionary business-builder. But it is also the most elusive and difficult to learn. We describe Creative Smarts here to acknowledge its role and importance in business creation and entrepreneurship, and also to identify and embrace this type of talent when you encounter it. If you do see it—grab it.

Put simply, people who are strong on the Creative Smarts dimension are those we usually describe as visionaries, idea generators, or innovators. How they got that way is less clear than the mechanism and habits behind other types of Smarts. We have argued that you can practice and learn Book Smarts, Street Smarts, and People Smarts. The Creative Smarts bucket is different.

How do people like Guy Laliberté, the founder of Cirque du Soleil, envision what he does as a new expression and redefinition of the "circus"? Or how did Steve Jobs see opportunities at Apple and Pixar that others did not? What was the force that led Sony's Akio Morita to decide that he needed to rebrand and position his company around how he wanted people to *feel* with his product? These and other inventors, game-changers, and maverick thinkers are people who possess the ability to "see around corners," to reframe their business definition (e.g., what really makes for a circus), and even to reshape entire industries. They do this using what is seemingly uncanny and intuitive Creative Smarts to posit what it is that will resonate with people.

Such creative forces and personalities are rare. We see and meet quite a few people who can generate ideas, but those who have *both* ideas that push boundaries *and* the ability to express their creativity into reality is what makes this group special. Fueled by a deep passion stemming from Heart and a capability from Creative Smarts, they are able to produce not just customer products and services, but customer *experiences* that often feel magical. People successful with their Creative Smarts often have Heart as a parallel (or even dominant) trait that guides their purpose and passion. With Heart leading the *why* behind what they do, their Creative Smarts expresses the *how* in new and unique ways.

Those with Creative Smarts often understand what consumers "don't know they don't know." This, of course, became a well-known quality associated with the late Steve Jobs, who was infamous for eschewing customer research in favor of what he felt he just knew Apple users would want.

As there are, almost by definition, few frameworks that can meaningfully augment your Creative Smarts, what do business-builders who have strong Creative Smarts possess that others lack? And what can we learn most from them?

Those with high Creative Smarts are phenomenal at sensing and interpreting patterns. How they research these patterns can be instructive. The Pixar team behind the movie *A Bug's Life* placed tiny cameras on top of Lego pieces and stationed them right in front of their studio in a patch of dirt, grass, and plants. The pieces had wheels and were taped to a stick to be pushed around the patch, a half-inch above the ground, to understand the world from a bug's perspective. Who *does* that stuff?

It is obviously important to any business venture to look at the world through new lenses and offer new ways of doing things. This requires bridging Book and Street Smarts with this more amorphous Creative Smarts. American psychobiologist Roger W. Sperry was among the first to propose that the mind has two distinct ways of thinking: a *right brain* that observes the world visually and holistically before breaking it down to the constituent parts; and a verbally oriented *left brain* that focuses on discrete pieces of information before assembling a more comprehensive view. Historically, we refer to these two modalities of thinking as *left-brain* and *right-brain* thinking, with the left analytical and the right more artistic. Younger business-builders often err on the side of left-brain thinking, while giving short shrift to the Creative Smarts) side, even though their right brains enable them to work in groups, use analogs from past personal experience or from the experience of others, and learn via visual cues.

Creative Smarts can also help leaders understand how a brand *feels*, especially if it needs a change. Sony was initially launched and gained momentum as the Tokyo Telecommunications Engineering Corporation, a real mouthful. Cofounder Akio Morita realized, however, that brand-name identification was as important as good products to the company's success. He wanted a name that would be easy to pronounce and easy to remember. His approach to the new name was about how it felt and resonated: it was made up from the Latin word *sonus*, which means "sound," and *sonny*, which he thought was a "friendly" term that also sounded like the sun. Most everyone around him thought he was crazy to change the name of a successful company, but in 1958, he opted for Sony, a decision that played out pretty well for the business.

Creative Smarts, then, is an inspiration source for the seed of a novel idea, innovation, or invention. With it comes an ability to push people into areas of new possibility and understanding. That Creative Smarts is something much more difficult to distill into habits to learn is part of its mystery and magic.

Is There Such a Thing as Too Much Smarts?

Is there such a thing as too much Smarts? We're not about to tell you that Smarts doesn't matter. But an entrepreneur will sometimes find she should simply dial back the Smarts.

To understand this, let's look at some of the key ways Smarts-dominant individuals are different. In the results of our E.A.T. survey (summarized in figure 3-1), Smarts-dominant individuals showed clear variances in how they responded to some of the most important questions when it comes to understanding how someone leads. Smarts-dominant entrepreneurs were almost five times more likely to attribute their success to "intellectual horsepower" over their "initiative to do things others were afraid to do." They were also more than three times more likely to report that friends would say they are "brilliant" as opposed to "bold." And there is no doubt that high-IQ folks know they have a quick mind—Smarts-dominant folks were almost five times more likely to believe their friends who say they have an "above-average IQ" compared with "above-

FIGURE 3-1

What Does It Mean to Be Smarts-Driven?

PERCENT WHO CHOSE THIS OPTION

SMARTS-DOMINANT

I'VE BEEN SUCCESSFUL THANKS TO:			SMARTS-DOMINANT	ALL OTHERS
My initiative to do things others were afraid to do	←·····→	My intellectual horsepower	93%	17%
My passion for what I do	←·····→	My mind	57%	32%

WHICH STATEMENT RESONATES MORE?				
It is important that I pursue continuous self-development	←·····→	It is important that I solve complex problems	57%	16%
I gut it out; most things can be resolved by action, effort, or time	←·····→	I think it out first; I can solve most things to which I apply my mind	79%	41%

MY FRIENDS WOULD BE MORE LIKELY TO SAY THAT:				
I am bold	←·····→	I am brilliant	86%	25%
I have above-average vision and passion	←·····→	I have above-average IQ	93%	22%

average vision and passion." Like many things, these strengths can also be a weakness.

For instance, an overdose of Book Smarts can prevent an entrepreneur from grasping the big picture. Steve Papa, founder of the software business Endeca, explains that his company employs highly skilled software developers who are now and again "too smart for their own good." They orient their products toward achieving a degree of complexity that they themselves would desire. In the end, though, 99 percent of their IT customers are in search of simplicity. Endeca risked alienating this market by emphasizing technological enhancements that most consumers found unnecessary. Fact was, the team's analytical brilliance was damaging its sales. "For a long time," recalls Papa, "we thought that those groups weren't getting where our software was going, but it was *we* who didn't understand what our software needed to be."

A Book Smarts entrepreneur must also cope with her overcritical instincts as she finds and tries to fix whatever holes there are in a plan: *What if there is a 2 percent chance that we're misinterpreting our results? What if our market is smaller than we think? What if a business with a similar purpose floundered in the past?* These are all valid concerns—but to get anywhere, entrepreneurs also have to be willing to take a leap of faith. Notes Papa, "The classic person who goes into management consulting . . . could tell me all the reasons why something won't work, but very often won't tell me the reasons why something can, or what you'd have to do to make it work." Approaching an uncertain possibility from the perspective that it *might* work allowed Papa to take an untraditional, untested approach as he built up his business. Soundly managing and leveraging Smarts helped Papa build a successful business: shortly after we spoke with Papa, Endeca was acquired by Oracle for approximately $1 billion.

Another take on the limitations of Book Smarts comes from Ajay Piramal, the chairman of Piramal Enterprises Limited, who transformed his family-run textile company into a highly successful group comprising Nicholas Piramal, India's fourth-largest pharmaceutical company; Morarjee Goculdas Spinning & Weaving; and Piramal Glass. "As an entrepreneur, one cannot go and live by what reports and analyses there are," Piramal says. "Everyone has access to that data. The Excel sheet will show everyone the same value—and then the entrepreneur must decide if the same '100' value can be made into '200' or more."[9]

Book Smarts isn't the only category that can overdo it. A Street Smart business-builder risks becoming overconfident that she can "feel" her way to success or use a past playbook that has repeatedly worked. We value experience mightily—yet we also recognize that today is not yesterday. Information emerges. Rules change. Among the critical factors in Endeca's success, concludes Steve Papa, is his own ability to adapt to economic disruptions and "the moving average of ideas." He adds, "There are people who are comfortable with change, and they will take in new information and quickly adapt their thinking, but there are others who will discredit it until they see enough of a pattern." That can mean sticking to traditional views until the opportunity to change slips through their fingers. You can't always wait for the business world to develop a clear new pattern—smart adaptation means not waiting to change until you have no other choice.

And the Winner Is . . . Pattern Recognition: Business Smarts

By now we hope you agree with us that Smarts—particularly classic IQ Smarts—is often overrated. After all, in their list of the most important HSGL traits, founders and early-stage business-builders ranked old-fashioned, classical IQ as coming in dead last in importance. Notes Kimbal Musk, "There are the high-IQ guys, and then there are the dodgers and weavers. It's like in basketball: you can have a guy who's seven feet tall, but the guy who is five-foot-six and who hustles can actually beat that guy. For most start-ups, you don't need a 200 IQ. You can have it in the low 100s, and you'll do just fine."

What *is* a requirement for business success is the deft amalgam of the four varieties of Smarts we have listed above, which come together to form what we call Business Smarts. Simply put, Business Smarts is the ability not only to mix and match the above qualities, but also to modify and moderate their volume depending on the person, people, situation, or environment in question.

Business Smarts may sound conscious, and shrewd, but it is not. It is intuitive and experiential, visionary and practical. By way of analogy, a chess-master is not necessarily aware of what skills and qualities he brings to a match. As he squares off against a random opponent, he has to consider everything he knows: the game; the manuals he has absorbed; the teachers he has learned from; the number of directions available for movement. Simultaneously he recalls opponents he has played against, the tactics and strategies he has memorized through trial and error, as well as the clock and the timer. Now he studies his opponent's body language, his grimace, or lack of expression; what his opponent's hand and brain may be doing; and his own likely next moves. At the same time, our chess master's own brain is sifting through patterns and smarts habits. It's now time to formulate a strategy. Will it be shocking or conventional, indirect or obvious?

In short, our chess master has to dial up and dial down his Book Smarts, Street Smarts, People Smarts, and Creative Smarts easily and quickly, while also summoning and applying habits he has learned over a lifetime.

In this same way, an individual gifted with Business Smarts can sniff out the big picture from among a multitude of patterns. Yet anyone in a leadership position knows that interpreting data patterns, observing business and environmental trends, and managing a broad spectrum of personal interactions is just the beginning. The Business Smart leader must also spot the patterns that lie *within* the patterns. While rapidly assessing the tenor and temperature of fast-flowing events, she must also fit individual goals with the central aim of the organization. Her goal is to identify and keep sight of the end game, while keeping every single short-term element of the company in motion. We can learn from Toyota, whose managers were famous for understanding the underlying patterns and causes of a situation by asking "Why?" five times.

What can you do to improve your Business Smarts? Observe the actions of others. Study books. Study people. Study art. Take a psychology course. Remain attentive to leadership decisions that you've gleaned from business articles.

Or, best of all, learn by doing. Sit at a desk. Size up your options. Take the plunge. Make a decision. Don't be afraid to fail, or make mistakes. Use failure as a stepping-stone, but don't make the same mistake twice. Continuously self-evaluate what works for you, and what doesn't. And read through the series of Wisdom Manifestos that we've included at the end of the book, which focus mostly on Business Smarts. We encourage you to tear out the pages—as long as you own the book.

Our guess? You're probably way smarter than you think you are.

CHAPTER IN SUMMARY

Smarts: IQ Is Only the Beginning

- Smarts: Smarts is all about recognizing patterns. It's about grasping macro and micro trends earlier and faster by connecting different observations and different types of smarts.

- The Types of Smarts: There's Book Smarts, Street Smarts, People Smarts, and Creative Smarts—which together make up Business Smarts and the pattern recognition within it.

- Book Smarts: Intelligence marked by innate analytical ability that makes for better, informed, objective, and fact-based decision making. Book Smarts matters more for business scaling in larger organizations than in start-ups.
  - Habits: An annual memo to the board with your top five priorities. Maniacal focus on input/leading indicator metrics versus output/lagging financial metrics. The key to better, shorter meetings.

- Street Smarts: The ability to bring practicality and momentum to a business, and using experience and common sense to get things done.
  - Habits: The *three-minute rule* highlights the importance of understanding the context in which your customer uses your product. The second Street Smarts habit is to "play stupid, win smart" by hitting our "mute" button more—pause, think, and then act, instead of reacting.

- People Smarts: Individuals with People Smarts can better sense and empathize with the people around them. Their intuitive comprehension of others' intentions allows them to better respond and better connect.
  - Habits: Know how to have critical conversations, triage and prioritize relationships with the 5 percent rule, and use intrinsic factors (e.g., a meaningful role) as much as (or even more than) extrinsic factors like pay to motivate people.

- Creative Smarts: Creative Smarts gives people the ability to conceptualize, innovate, and grasp patterns that others don't, generating new and unexpected ideas. Creative Smarts tends to appear in more right-brain-oriented individuals. The provenance of this skill set is as unclear as its impact on a business is profound.

- Too Much Smarts: Smarts-driven entrepreneurs can sometimes fail to grasp the big picture, focusing too much on the details and sometimes becoming "precisely incorrect." Smarts are essential, but in the end, entrepreneurs have to be willing to take a leap of faith.

- The Perfect Blend: Each type of Smarts comes with its own risks and shortcomings. Business Smarts is about mixing and matching the different types of Smarts, modifying their levels in accord with the situation at hand, and applying the appropriate strategies and proven practices. Business Smarts individuals see not just the patterns but also the big pictures they form.

4

GUTS:
How to Initiate, Endure, and Evolve

Entrepreneurship is often a lonely endeavor, marked by repeated rejection and failure. Look deeper into the "overnight" business success story of any founder or team, and you'll usually uncover a multiyear, circuitous journey made up of extreme highs and lows.

Launching anything new means a commitment to swimming (at least for a while) in a sea of ambiguity. This can be terrifying. Many business leaders spend most of their waking hours physically or psychologically alone, convinced that no one understands their ideas. This isn't *normal*. Most humans are drawn naturally to the status quo. People generally prefer the established and time-tested routine as opposed to the potentially disruptive plans or visions of a founder.

This is why Guts is such an essential trait for business-building success. Guts gives you the thick skin and fortitude to initiate, to ignore whatever criticism you're likely to hear, to persevere, to stand confidently behind an idea, and to know when to take swift, necessary action. Visionary business-builders tell us that their job is to transport others to a future that they glimpsed months or years earlier—and to close the time gap between the present and the future as quickly as possible. People with a high Guts-Heart constitution seem best at managing and inspiring others *during* that time gap so that it collapses faster. Indeed, the Guts-Heart combination is among the most common for those who start businesses. No enterprise becomes great without an ahead-of-the-pack, lone-wolf leader who dares to disregard conventions.

Take Mike Yavonditte, for example, former CEO of Quigo (a contextual ad-targeting network that directly competed with Google's AdSense) and now founder of Hashable. Talking to us in front of a glass wall where we could see the engineers of Hashable at work, he shared his perspectives on Guts. "We were competing against Google every day, and that took Guts. A lot of people said we were crazy. We had to go in there, day in and day out, for a long time, against a big competitor. We didn't know for sure if we would make it, and we had to persevere. I think perseverance is a critical characteristic that connects successful people."[1] This attitude worked well for Yavonditte—after turning down an acquisition offer for over $150 million (to the consternation of many involved in the business), he pressed on and eventually sold the company for over $350 million.

"Building a company is filled with a lot of ups and downs, a lot of disappointment," says Yavonditte. "A lot of things go wrong, and a lot of people will disappoint you, and the market will disappoint you, and the way people react to your product or service will disappoint you." What's essential, he says, is the willingness to keep working and persisting.

That's why business-builders need Guts. In this chapter, we describe different types of Guts, discuss the need for Guts at different stages of a business, and highlight the lessons of some Guts-driven entrepreneurs and business-builders.

An Inside Job

Trusting our Gut, says heart surgeon and TV host Dr. Mehmet Oz, is in fact a physical and neurological reality. When we're feeling stressed or uneasy, our gastrointestinal nerve endings give us instinctual advice about how we should act and react. During these situations, our "guts" work in concert with the primitive region of our brains associated with instinctual responses. Smarts-dominant individuals, who tend to process information in the more advanced frontal cortices of their brains, sometimes need to learn how to dial down their own complex decision making, especially during moments of crisis and decisiveness. Oz himself made a Guts-driven decision to shift his focus from the operating room to the television studio—a move that was not at all obvious for one with such a stellar and respected surgical career.

Guts is the critical trait that helps us control fear. Make no mistake: intrepid or gutsy individuals are hardly fearless; they are simply better than the rest of the population at coping with, and even thriving in, fear-based environments. A gutsy individual isn't someone who doesn't feel fear; he's someone who acts *despite* his fear.

Alpha personalities—adrenaline junkies, high-frequency traders, serial entrepreneurs—appear to be born with a need for high-risk, high-stakes scenarios and behaviors. Other Guts-dominant individuals have developed a capacity for risk tolerance over time. Some argue that the best entrepreneurs are not so much risk seekers as they are risk tolerators or risk mitigators, people who are good at recognizing risks and then managing them. Their uncanny stoicism and presence of mind allow them to show

Guts Defined

Guts /guhts/ *noun* 1 : the courage to make things happen with the will to act; specifically at critical moments of initiation, endurance, and evolution

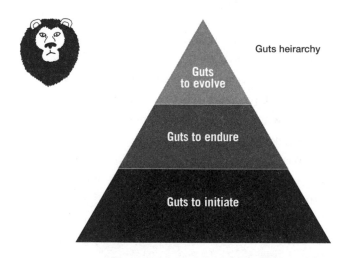

Guts heirarchy

leadership during high-stress situations, whether it's turning around a decaying company or reinventing themselves after a traumatic career setback. We hold the highest respect for Guts-dominant individuals because they move forward when others just stand there. We can learn a lot from them.

During the beginnings of the dot-com boom, Intel cofounder Andy Grove wrote a book called *Only the Paranoid Survive*, arguing that great business-builders and developers *should* fear competition, product launch dates, cash-burn, their struggle to attract the best talent, and many other things.[2] This kind of paranoia breeds the fortitude that encourages confidence, resilience, and presence of mind. (Again, courage isn't about banishing fear, but rather about transforming negativity into productivity.)

That said, all Guts are not created equal. In our survey sample of entrepreneurs, we found that approximately 35 percent possessed Guts as a primary or secondary trait. As we followed up with interviews, we found that among these leaders' qualities was not only the baseline ability to initiate action, but the capacity to persevere and also to transform themselves and their companies when necessary. An implicit Guts hierarchy emerged (see "Guts Defined"): many people demonstrated the baseline ability to take action in the face of risk, fewer exhibited relentless persistence against challenges, and fewer still exhibited the ability to recognize the uncomfortable need to evolve.

We explore each one of these characteristics below.

The Guts to Initiate

Are you a bond or an equity? Are you willing to give up certainty to pursue something with meaning and purpose? Or will your practical, realistic side impel you toward more conservative choices? It takes Guts to begin something, both at the earliest stages of business formation and at the later, slower-growth stages—when the need for change is evident, but too few people can make that change happen. Entrepreneurs and business-builders need the minimum baseline of Guts to be able to initiate and take action. The Guts to Initiate enables the ultimate leap of faith when little evidence suggests your venture will bear fruit.

Guts are the foundation of optimistic leadership. Founders must lead with the vision that they are doing something great. Confidence, passion, and conviction are contagious qualities. Armed with high Heart and optimism, it becomes easier to initiate. Not to mention that a person armed with passion can manage his fear more easily.

The Guts to Endure

The Guts to Endure is about withstanding the test of time. Business leaders who persevere recognize a core paradox in the journey of business-building: the delicate balance between refusing to accept failure and embracing it when it appears.

From the perspective of the Guts-driven, people need to adopt the Vince Lombardi attitude of "hating losing" more than "loving winning." They should also develop the capacity to elevate themselves above losses with humility and reflection. The optimal mind-set? *Failure is not an option, but a reality.*

The Guts to Endure is also about remaining strong and resolute in your vision when you know you are right (and to hell with the naysayers). Do you have the resilience to stick with it—and the strategic capacity to rise up when you are down?

The Guts to Evolve

The Guts to Evolve is the ability of people to enact change within themselves—to alter their opinions, eat crow, and respond appropriately to new information without allowing their own pride to slant or prejudice the facts.

The Guts to Evolve sits atop our Guts pyramid. The people and plans necessary to start and prove a business are almost always different from the people and plans needed to scale and adapt that business to the next level. At these critical business junctures, individuals with the Guts to Evolve are able to embrace their inner chameleon. They put their success at risk in order to break through the threshold and lead across the next chapter of a business's growth. Becoming a chameleon doesn't mean changing your color hourly or daily; it means remaining attentive and responsive to environmental conditions and cyclical thresholds. At these critical thresholds of a firm's growth, those with the Guts to Evolve are able to change the direction of a company in the face of new competitors or new consumer attitudes, or they are able to recognize the need to change themselves out of leadership for the greater good of the business.

Some Guts-dominant readers will find that they fall into two or even all three categories of our Guts hierarchy. Others will feel they mostly exhibit one. Alone, or in any combination, these categories forecast how Guts-dominant individuals will perform in situations of stress, difficulty, or uncertainty. We explore each category below in further detail.

The Guts to Initiate: The Baseline for Getting Things Done

Entrepreneurs who profile strongly in the Guts dimension are more at ease challenging the status quo, setting trends, and placing their reputations on the line. Their credo might well be: *Action, not inaction, and not reaction.*

If you're thinking, "That is *definitely* not me," pause for a second. Consider the times when you actually did put something at risk: your coursework as you pursued a dorm-room enterprise, your comfort zone as you moved to a new city across the country for a new job, or your pride as you tried to chat up strangers who might not be as interested in you as you were in them. Many of you likely have started or joined a venture in which you hold deep passion—taking a risk and trading off against more conventional career paths. It turns out that those who follow Robert Frost's path less taken do tend to build stronger Guts. Just as green shoots might portend the tallest of trees, so do these actions reveal the potential to develop some serious Guts.

In our interview with Mehmet Oz, he reflected on the moments in the operating room when he has had to make go/no-go decisions. A heart transplant is not working, the EKG is flatlining, and applying a thumb's pressure to the heart can only slow the bleeding for so long. Now what? *First*, Oz stresses, *you take an action, and take it quickly*. Pondering options and alternatives does no one any good (particularly the patient). You can learn to live with taking an action that leads to a mistake far better than you can live with taking no action at all. Inaction almost always leads to failure, while making a decision promises at the very least the possibility of a positive outcome.

Thus, this foundation level of our Guts hierarchy framework, the Guts to Initiate, is the most common and essential trait of Guts-driven individuals. If you are Guts-dominant, you will always prioritize decision making over indecision. Even after considering worst-case scenarios, you will invariably decide it is worth jumping in.

The world is overweighted with idea generators and underweighted with people actually willing to execute their ideas. Even during the dot-com boom in the mid- to late 1990s, surprisingly few of those enrolled at top business schools across the country were launching new companies, given the large number who professed excitement for new ideas. By Tony's recollection, in 1998, two years before the dot-com peak, the number of Harvard Business School second-year students starting their own ventures came to less than ten in a class of about nine hundred.

The sustained boom in China and other BRIC countries (Brazil, Russia, India, and China) in the early 2000s was another such phenomenon. Lots of people saw and commented on those countries' shifts and explosive growth patterns. Yet how many rearranged their careers to take advantage of their insights?

Each of this book's authors took decisive actions at pivot points of major technology and emerging market shifts, with life-changing consequences. While still in business school, Tony started ZEFER, a pioneering Internet strategy and Web-development firm that within five years had grown to more than $100 million in revenues and nearly a thousand people. Dick, after spending his career in the newspaper business, saw the impact of the Internet and decided to get his company, Thomson, out of newspapers and embrace the new era of providing digital services for professionals. Over the next decade, that decision would lead to about $30 billion of value creation. Tsun-yan, after years of being a successful senior director of McKinsey in North America, decided in 2000 to move to Singapore to become a leader in developing the McKinsey's Asia practice—enabling him to build close relationships with people who are now among the most prominent business leaders and entrepreneurs on the planet.

The Guts to Initiate is often highly correlated with Heart-dominance. A high Guts-Heart profile, which translates into an individual with high passion and determination, is a powerful combination. If people possess high Heart—and therefore deep-seated passion for their ideas—they find it easier to take action. That said, Heart alone does not compel an individual to action. We all remember the secret crushes and furtive loves of our adolescence. How often did we do anything about them? The "boy meets girl, boy falls in love with girl, but does not tell girl" (or vice versa) storyline of countless saccharine movies clearly reflects a truth of life! It applies in business, too.

Dan Pallotta is a great example of an entrepreneur with the Guts to Initiate. He went from organizing fundraising events at Harvard College to creating cross-country cycling rides that collectively raised over $300 million for charity. Pallotta TeamWorks, the for-profit entity that organized the events, also brought a controversial private-sector model to the social sphere.

In his 2009 book, *Uncharitable*, Pallotta identifies various "rules" of the nonprofit sector that limit its potential, including low wages, extreme risk aversion, minimal spending on advertising and promotion, and the unavailability of venture capital or equity investments.[3] Pallotta had the Guts to initiate a creative, game-changing approach to charitable fundraising, and to stick with it despite heavy criticism of the attendant costs (including Pallotta's professional fees). His basic premise and model was to bring private-sector-style salaries, innovation, and capital investment to the nonprofit sector.[4]

Another example of an entrepreneur with the Guts to Initiate is Kishore Biyani, the founder of Future Group in India. Inspired by the large bazaars in Mumbai, Biyani wanted to create "the familiarity of an Indian bazaar . . . in a modern environment." He was met with dismissal and ridicule when he went into business, he told the Dubai-based newspaper *The National*: "Brands never wanted to supply to us, banks never wanted to extend lending," then added, "but that's the fun." In 1996, the biggest stores in Kolkata were four thousand square feet. He convinced the owner of a ten-thousand-square-foot space to rent it to him, and soon established the first Pantaloons department store. He quickly tried even bigger stores, with the first Big Bazaar opening in 2001. Now he's known as India's "king of retail."

Over the years, we have encountered two "false-positive" types of entrepreneurs. The first is one who has convinced himself he is an entrepreneur but who lacks an idea (high Smarts, little Heart); while the second is a passionate idealist who continually cogitates over ideas without taking action and is the first to criticize ideas in the market with "I had that idea first, but . . ."

The bottom line: Ideas mean nothing without practical action, which is why we set the Guts to Initiate as the threshold requirement of Guts.

The Guts to Endure: Persistence and Resilience in the Face of Uncertainty

Think of the Guts to Initiate as the willingness to run a hundred-meter dash. If you win, the gold medal is yours. If you lose—well, at least the whole race took less than fifteen seconds and the results were instantaneous.

In contrast, the Guts to Endure—the second level of our Guts hierarchy—is akin to a grueling road race.

One especially brutal race is the hundred-mile Leadville Ultramarathon, which takes place among the high-altitude Rocky Mountain peaks that surround the former mining town of Leadville, Colorado. Chances are you've never heard of this race, and it's even less likely that you'd be interested in running it. Yes: A hundred-mile run. Through the Rocky Mountains. At elevations as high as 14,400 feet. On your marks, get set, go!

The athletes who show up in Leadville every summer aren't competing for glory, fame, or a multimillion-dollar Nike contract. No, they epitomize Guts to Endure. With or without a first-place medal, the personal journey and accomplishment (training for and completing this footrace) is reward by itself. And this particular mind-set is what Guts to Endure is all about. An athlete with the staying power and stamina to run a hundred-mile race and an entrepreneur who spends a decade navigating the up-and-down journey of business-building have a lot in common.

A key here is the ability to see that a larger goal makes the short-term sacrifice worth it. Guts to Endure has less to do with eliminating fear than it does with maintaining perspective on expectations. You cannot succeed in sales, for example, unless you have the thick skin and perspective to realize you'll be wasting a lot of your time and effort. (Business schools would do well to spend more time teaching this core skill.)

Having Guts is not about being blind to risk taking, but having risk *awareness*, as the story of one of Canada's wealthiest families, and their quest to develop the financial district of Canary Wharf in London, attests.

Paul Reichmann of Olympia & York is a storied business-builder who set out to transform entire neighborhoods or sections of cities. Some of his early bets worked out spectacularly well. Reichmann's First Canadian Place in Toronto, completed in 1976 and covering an entire city block, contains Canada's tallest skyscraper, still the defining edifice of downtown Toronto's financial district. Next came the breathtaking takeover of a large swath of prime New York office buildings in 1977, not long after the Big Apple had almost gone bankrupt, then the development of the World Financial Center complex in lower Manhattan.

But the story of Paul Reichmann that embodies the Guts-dominant leader comes from his mammoth transformation project in London's then-derelict docklands—Canary Wharf. Hatched in 1988, Canary Wharf, which spans more than one hundred acres, ran into difficulties from the start, including local opposition, the reluctance of tenants to relocate, and the absence of a transportation infrastructure. Reichmann's troubles were further compounded by a deep recession in New York City, where Olympia & York had become Manhattan's largest landlord.

Olympia & York went bankrupt in 1992, erasing Reichmann's property portfolio, most of his personal fortune, and his deity status in the business world. Undaunted, he led a consortium that took Canary Wharf over again in 1995, took it public in 1999, and finally saw the development realize its promise as the new Jubilee Underground line connected it to the rest of the London and the booming financial industry quickly occupied shiny new building after shiny new building.

In 2004, the seventy-four-year-old Reichmann fought to take Canary Wharf private, only to lose out to Morgan Stanley. Two years later he rose again, and at age seventy-six, launched a new investment fund of $4 billion. Although he was able to regain an 8.45 percent stake in Canary Wharf, he eventually lost most of that, too, after the financial crisis in 2009.[5]

Once, during a meeting that Tsun-yan attended, Reichmann asked everyone present to come up with an amount of money he or she would be happy to live with. (His own number was shockingly low). "Assuming we could set that amount aside to satisfy our desires," he said, "what would you do with the rest of the money? How might you approach the same business decision with the money you have over and above that amount?" One can begin to understand why Reichmann has so much courage to act in pursuit of his vision. Both then and now, his perspective has been that business-builders should risk anything over and above that number to pursue and sustain their dreams.

Most "overnight successes" suffer from amnesia about the years of trial and tribulation that led them to that instant success.

The Guts to Evolve: Adapting to the Environment

The peppered moth is perhaps not the most obvious choice of a model for winning entrepreneurship. These winged pests, native to the United Kingdom, pause on tree trunks to rest. Their hues were once predominantly white or off-white, with darker speckles on their wings. This coloring was camouflage: trees in England were often covered with light-colored lichen, and by spreading their wings while they rested, peppered moths could become nearly invisible to birds and other predators. A very, very unlucky .01 percent of the peppered moth population, though, carried the dominant gene for dark grey wing color.

Then, in the nineteenth century, a funny thing happened in England. The Industrial Revolution was in full swing, and in the countryside around industrial hubs like London and Manchester, tree trunks were soon coated in dark soot. In the blink of an evolutionary eye, the peppered moth's dominant camouflage pattern became a serious liability. While the majority of the moth population in the area suffered, the tiny fraction of the group that carried the allele for dark wings survived and multiplied. In fact, they survived so well that by 1895, scientists reported that areas around Manchester were home to a population that was roughly 98 percent dark-colored. The peppered moth as a species survived a potentially catastrophic exogenous change to its environment by *evolving*.

Obviously, key differences exist between winged insects and entrepreneurs. For one thing, entrepreneurs do not (typically) reproduce twice per year, nor do they naturally evolve with external stimuli—although as venture capitalists, we wish they would! But savvy entrepreneurs know that in order to survive, they must have the self-awareness to adapt to environmental changes, and sometimes make very drastic shifts (for one example, see "Hold Steady to the Anchor: Guts to Evolve and Newspapers"). New information, new technologies, new regulations, new competition, and other industry shifts will always be around the corner. Hence the need for the top level of our Guts hierarchy, the Guts to Evolve.

Dick Harrington on Holding Steady to the Anchor: Guts to Evolve and Newspapers

The end of newspapers became apparent to me around 1998 on a skiing trip in Vermont. A man told me he owned an auto dealership that was beginning to see the negative impacts of customers gleaning pricing information from the Internet. He talked about people's unwillingness to negotiate, as early online auto research content and tools provided alternative sources for cars, including information on which options to buy and not to buy, along with other proconsumer negotiation tactics.

It suddenly became clear: soon people would not just be researching cars online but actually would be buying cars online, which meant they would be researching and buying other products online, too. Advertising now in newspapers and other print venues would move online. In that moment, I knew that newspapers would soon become a thing of the past. It was time to get out.

The decision to sell Thomson's newspaper business did not come without a level of emotion and trepidation. The Thomson Corporation, of which I was CEO, was built on the success of newspapers. Moreover, newspapers represented the spirit and soul of the founding family. The company had grown from a single paper to the ownership of 250 newspapers around the world. They were at the very core of its identity.

The prospective loss of Thomson's newspapers was not something to be taken lightly from a financial standpoint, either. At the time, our business was growing at roughly 9 percent a year, at a time when most other North American newspapers were growing at 2 to 4 percent. Several people on the board of directors were convinced that it was crazy to sell when we were doing so well—why not hold on a bit longer?

So there was a level of Guts, Smarts, and Luck—not to mention careful planning—in discussing the sale with our family owner, who was by nature a sentimentalist. But however bold my act appeared, my style of Guts was and is anything but impulsive. The world was at that time and is today too complex to simply pull a Guts feeling from the sky. Guts needs an anchor, and my anchor has always been the constant absorption of industry and customer information. So in this sense it is the combination of Guts and Smarts in action. I had carefully examined the Internet's projected growth and the shift in our customers' preferences, and once I decided the future was not in newspapers I knew I needed to stick firmly to that decision: put another way, if you've dropped the anchor, you need to hold steady to it, or you'll have a disaster on your hands.

We all had to fight our fear. We were taking a leap of faith. Though we had plotted the expected trajectory, we didn't really know exactly where we would land. And even as we dubbed ourselves an "e-information company" (gosh, everything was "e" at the time), we didn't completely know what that would mean—it was all still fascinatingly new. As CEO, my own career was also on the line, as I would now have been held personally responsible had the sellout failed. The solution for me was again to simply commit myself to my belief and decision and to force myself into an out-of-body release of my doubts. Once we had sold, we had sold. All we could do was hold steady to the anchor and not look back.

We ended up having great support from the family and shareholders, since we showed that we hadn't allowed our love of the businesses to blind us to the right path. Most companies and business-builders inevitably will come to a crossroads when they need to think about whether to redefine themselves and take a leap into the unknown.

I was speaking at an event recently when a man came up to me and introduced himself. "Dick," he told me, "I tell people that you're the smartest newspaper person I know."

I looked at him in surprise. "But we sold them."

He smiled. "That's right."

A very fine line exists between perseverance and stubbornness. To know when to stand firm, and when to adapt is one of the most crucial qualities a business-builder can possess, and a hallmark of the Guts to Evolve.

In hindsight, it's a cinch: we dub someone who sticks to his guns despite widespread criticism and derision "determined," "strong-willed," or "visionary with conviction." However, when someone is wrong about his idea or strategy, we call him "stubborn," "close-minded," and "just plain stupid." Because entrepreneurs are always attempting to introduce new ideas, by definition they lead at the outset with a stubborn, contrarian quality. What's hard is to realize when they need to change course or accept that they are just plain wrong.

The companies that don't survive are the ones that don't adapt their practices and products to environmental shifts. The failure to change internally when a start-up begins to grow—failure to scale—is just one such example. Another is our tendency to rely on what has worked in the past, or even to fall in love with an idea or business. As many have warned us, and as we have experienced in our own past businesses, you should never fall in love with a business idea. Sometimes you need to "trade out" just as quickly as you "traded in."

This courage to depart from past success and evolve to meet future needs is not limited to entrepreneurs. Corporate titans face the same challenge, and most don't fare any better. The list of those that failed after their initial success, then requiring a departure and new evolution, is very long. Just to name a few: Polaroid, Kodak, Xerox (until Anne Mulcahy became CEO), Motorola, and IBM (until Louis Gerstner came in) all faced enormous declines when past successes turned into emotional roadblocks. J.P. Morgan took an enormous risk to evolve in the 1970s, at the height of its success. The firm had been a pure-play commercial lender to any business that needed credit. In an effort to evolve, the firm did two things. First, it narrowly focused on just its top one hundred clients. Second, it expanded from credit into investment banking and advisory services. J.P. Morgan was one of the rare companies that, at the height of its success, wagered it all for a different kind of future, despite questions about what the change would mean for its culture and what it would require of its talent.

During its fourteen-year existence, Athenahealth has passed through multiple pivots, storms, and triumphs, among them going through the headwind of the dot-com nuclear winter and emerging stronger, as eventually confirmed with one of the most successful IPOs of 2007. Like the Thomson transformation story presented in "Dick Harrington on Holding Steady to the Anchor," Athenahealth is a case study for the Guts to Evolve. Athenahealth began life in 1997 as about a dozen obstetric centers in San Diego with midwives delivering some two thousand babies a year. Just one year after founding, however, it became apparent to company cofounder Jonathan Bush and his team that owning health practices was not going to be a good business model. They were not completely sure of the right direction, but knew they had gone into the business to try and offer more efficient, and accessible, clinical care. The team decided that the best opportunity to realize its broader vision would be to shift from clinical care to offering Web-based medical billing and practice management software. Athenahealth divested its clinics and, despite some heavyweight competition from the likes of GE and Siemens, Bush and his team pushed forward believing that they could create a simpler, more standard solution. This shift was not easy. There were debates with VCs and even some months when the senior team had to go without salary. In the end, resilience, acceptance, learning, and evolution from some failures allowed Athenahealth to develop a suite of Web-based revenue management services and collection and electronic medical record solutions. At the time of writing, Athenahealth has had over forty-seven consecutive quarters of revenue growth, with nearly $250 million in annual revenue, thirteen hundred employees, and a market capitalization of $2 billion.[6] Not bad for a company unsure of its initial direction.

Stubbornness is great when you are right, but hell when you are wrong.

Manifesting Guts

As we put together our Guts hierarchy pyramid, we observed two principal ways in which Guts manifests itself: (1) episodically, during critical moments of truth that require decisive go/no-go decisions, and (2) longitudinally, over periods that require enormous perseverance. In business, when enterprise leaders are faced with the need to make a call and then live by that action, the above represent the two most frequently required types of Guts-oriented decisions. An example of the first—punctuated manifestation of Guts—might be: do we walk away from our biggest client, who now wants to enforce onerous terms? N. R. Narayana Murthy at Infosys did exactly that. An example of the second—longitudinally applied Guts—might be the Athenahealth team, whose persistence only increased in the face of failure and outsized competitors.

The key to long-term success, as we see it, is a balance of fast-twitch and slow-twitch Guts. The very best business leaders we know of possess the ability to act with the right instincts (with an eerily serene presence of mind during difficult go/no-go decisions), and to persevere through long, challenging periods of sustained volatility. We use the evolutionary biology term *punctuated equilibrium* to characterize the entrepreneurial journey: long periods of stasis (that require great perseverance) punctuated by moments of critical decision making that can either elevate a company to its next level or sink it to its demise.

The Guts You've Got and the Guts You Can Get: What Astronauts, High-Performance Athletes, and Heart Surgeons Can Teach Us in Business

What makes for a gutsy person? Can Guts be developed? Can Guts be predicted?

The willingness to take risks is born of a combination of elements. Your personality, your experiences, your "training" to deal with risk, and your support network all factor into your readiness to accept and embrace the risks that entrepreneurship requires. As Malvolio said in Shakespeare's *Twelfth Night*, "Some are born great, some achieve greatness, and others have greatness thrust upon them." In this respect, greatness and gutsiness are similar. Some individuals are born with a natural tendency toward gutsy behavior, some absorb it growing up, and others learn it during moments of reckoning.

Nature

External factors aside, some individuals are quite simply more risk hungry than others. While you cannot choose what degree of Guts you're born with, it can help to know if you're naturally fearless, genetically risk averse, or somewhere in between.

Perhaps you're more likely to analyze risks carefully, perform more research, or break the mold socially. These are all positive attributes; but at the risk of repeating ourselves, the baseline for entrepreneurial Guts is the willingness to take a risk. In the course of screening businesses in our day jobs as venture capitalists and advisers, we are principally screening people and their propensities for being strong business-builders. A big part of that is whether we feel that there is a natural fire in the belly, a desire to make something happen, and a need to *share* in that risk. (We get wary when people tell us they need to continue to have a certain level of guaranteed income with upside equity.)

There is often a correlation between strong Heart and strong Guts. Our research found that over two-thirds of Guts-dominant founders were Heart subdominant, and that nearly half of Heart-dominant founders were Guts subdominant. Believing in one's purpose and challenging oneself to achieve it are mutually reinforcing factors. Looked at another way: if there is Heart behind the idea, the "payoff" of pursuing it is larger than just the financial outcome, so the very risk/reward calculation done by a Heart-Guts-oriented person is skewed toward taking the chance, since the reward has an intrinsic component that makes it more desirable.

Nurture and Context

Risk tolerance is not an immutable quality. By placing themselves in certain targeted environments, business-builders can train themselves to be smarter, or more comfortable, with risk taking.

Early-life experiences play a part in shaping future risk takers, too. Your parents' attitudes toward work and rewards, and their ability to provide you with modest or comfortable means, were critical factors in your Guts, drive, and motivation to succeed. In this case, less is probably more. Approximately 65 percent of the billionaires on the *Forbes* list began with relatively nothing, monetarily speaking.[7]

Positive educational and early childhood experiences with entrepreneurship also play a substantial role. Did parents, friends, or teachers encourage you to learn the value of a dollar by starting a small business—a lemonade stand, a snack kiosk, a paper route, snow shoveling, or any other simple "kid business"?

80 percent of Guts-dominant founders had ventures as children.

Business-building is a journey. The more miles you travel, the more corners that you see around and explore, and the greater the number of critical decisions that accompany that journey, the greater your comfort will be with risk. A large acquisition or sale that was fear inducing the first time around eventually becomes almost second nature after you have been in that movie a few times. Those who have the opportunity to manage through a crisis, a challenging postmerger integration, a reset or turnaround of a business, or any other business challenge gain invaluable perspective. In short, the greater your experience, the more comfortable you will become with endeavors that people on the outside perceive as high-risk.

Training

Certain professions outside of entrepreneurship self-select for Guts-dominant individuals: the police force, the military, mining, astronauts, and surgery, to name just a few. But these professions have also developed training programs that can help individuals better prepare for setbacks and worst-case scenarios.

Practice leads to risk reduction. The training of commercial air pilots; NASA's training program; the risk-mitigation strategies and programs that large corporations adopt—how can some of these training practices be applied to smaller, faster-growing businesses?

As an entrepreneur, you will likely have to deal with the management equivalent of at least one failed space shuttle booster rocket. Astronauts train for years to handle this and other emergencies. How are they trained to handle go/no-go scenarios? How much is physical? How much is mental? A few interesting patterns emerged from our conversations with Guts-dominant individuals like the former astronaut Scott Parazynski (see "The Engineering Approach to Fear: A Conversation with Scott Parazynski" below) and the sailor Steve Callahan, who survived over seventy days stranded at sea (see "Survival of the Fittest: A Conversation with Steve Callahan").

Worst-Case Scenario Planning. You can gain psychological comfort by envisioning and understanding what can go wrong. Very often, the perceived risk of a situation outweighs the actual risk, leading to irrational behavior. The authors have often counseled young, highly risk-averse business school graduates about starting new ventures. We often ask: *What do you believe is your worst-case scenario? If you attempt to launch your start-up for two years and it fails, can you still secure the more conservative consulting, brand management, or banking job you're now considering?* Typically, the answer was yes. Thus, the ability to pursue a risk-filled endeavor becomes more palatable when graduates understand both the shelf life of the credibility of their degrees and the logical flaw in thinking that their second choice will disappear if they pursue their first choice.

The Engineering Approach to Fear: A Conversation with Scott Parazynski

Dr. Scott Parazynski, a veteran of five space shuttle flights and seven spacewalks, is the only person to have flown in space *and* summited Mt. Everest. He's now chief technology officer and chief medical officer at the Methodist Hospital Research Institute in Houston.

What role does Guts play in your life?

People think, "He is a daredevil." I can't tell you how incorrect that is! I am an extremely careful risk manager. Before I approached that *Hubble* servicing mission, I understood how every electron in that spacecraft might fail. With knowledge and training, anyone has the confidence to approach higher-risk environments.

Can entrepreneurs be defined less as "risk takers" than "risk mitigators"?

Yes. Entrepreneurs love adrenaline, but to be successful, they also have to be risk mitigators. You have to think hard about celebrating the hero firefighter who jumps into a burning building where the chances of saving someone are very low to nil, and the firefighter who assesses that by saving another person's life he is putting everyone else around at risk. The successful entrepreneur can weigh risks and rewards at the same time.

How pragmatic is your approach to tough challenges?

I take more of an engineering approach to fear and challenges. I think that folks who do so tend to be very successful.[8]

Training for Common Crises. In the business-building world, the situations are usually not as sudden, or as life-or-death, as the real-world examples of individuals fighting the challenges of space or the ocean. But surviving in the real world and the business world often feels the same. Both can be emotional and draining. Our advice? Prepare for crises by thinking in advance about what you'd do in various difficult situations: abruptly losing a key employee (what is your succession plan?); having your technology fail on you (do you have a redundancy plan?); needing to let go of several people to preserve cash (what are best practices on process and communications?); and responding to an aggressive takeover (how do you best negotiate or navigate out?). Knowing what some of these key crises and crossroads might be (we will discuss these later) will increase your Guts to Endure.

Support and Relationship Network

Knowing you can rely on a network of friends, family, and loved ones permits you to take risks you might not otherwise consider. Your relationship network serves the triple duty of social network, empathy group, and informal board of accountability (for instance, when you tell your closest friends and family members that you plan to do something, your fear of letting them down makes you more likely to carry through). Positive behavior change is often most influenced by a peer network, and in a similar fashion the support and accountability afforded by a group committed to seeing you succeed is one of the most important soft assets for any business-builder.

Survival of the Fittest: A Conversation with Steve Callahan

In January 1982, naval architect and sailor Steve Callahan spent seventy-six days stranded at sea after what was likely a whale rammed the self-built boat he was sailing alone from the Canary Islands to Antigua.

What is the "survivor" mind-set?

In the movie *Apollo 13*, the engineers keep shooting down ideas on how to fix the spacecraft. Finally, one blurts out, "I don't care what it was *designed* to do. What is it *capable* of doing?" That epitomizes the survivor mind-set.

How were you prepared for survival?

Worst-case-scenario planning was part of my preparation. A crisis is more chaotic than training can ever be, but training can at least help you know what critical steps to take. One of my favorite expressions is "Murphy was an optimist." You have to address challenges with whatever you have at your disposal.

What thought kept you strong?

If I couldn't control my reality, I could try to affect it, and that, combined with a little luck, would help me survive. I developed a daily survival routine to help [normalize] the experience.

Moreover, the people closest to you are the ones most likely to feel the effects of your entrepreneurial zeal. Your close friends, significant other, and family will be the ones most affected if you spend your waking hours writing code, recruiting new team members, raising money, or building prototypes in a basement or barren office. It is critical that your support network understand the business-building activity you are pursuing—less for the technical details than to appreciate the sacrifices and likely risks involved.

Mentors who have had their own entrepreneurial experiences are critical nodes in the support network. They can offer advice and wisdom based on their own struggles and successes, and ask instructive questions. Above all, mentors mirror and model behaviors that high-risk situations require. Sure, young leaders can learn lessons elsewhere, but nothing leaves quite so indelible an impression as observing up-close as a mentor displays the courage to act, endure, and evolve—and inspires young leaders to do the same.

To this end, a business-builder's personal relationships are of enormous importance. Whether you are starting your own firm, helping to evolve a start-up into a full-fledged business, or stepping in to save a failing brand, your network of supporters will both provide you with emotional strength and help you to perform your job better when things get tough. Studies show conclusively that individuals with stronger relationship networks live healthier, happier lives. Positive and negative behavior changes take place more often through peer-based networks than via other mechanisms. Those confidants and quiet cheerleaders who encourage entrepreneurs during the highs and lows of business-building aren't just nice to have. They're essential.

Finally, you can enhance your own propensity for Guts if you partner up with others who are willing either to join the journey or unequivocally support it. When Tony decided to start a company while in business school, the willingness peers eager to join in created the confidence that camaraderie often ignites. The initial team you build is obviously the relationship network most directly related to your business endeavor. But from there, consider concentric circles of support: family, mentors, close friends, and relevant industry and business contacts. Learn to openly communicate your stresses, challenges, and successes. At the same time, don't let others determine your path, as peer-based risk aversion among friends can be contagious. People who are following more conservative paths often want to justify their personal decisions and may subconsciously discourage your entrepreneurial journey.

What Are the Big Crossroad Decisions You Will Face?

We close this chapter with a handful of the most common crossroad decisions that business-builders and entrepreneurs face—pivot points that test one's Guts to Initiate, Guts to Endure, and Guts to Evolve. Know them before they happen, and you'll be more effective when they occur.

Crossroad: The Need to Pivot on the Original Vision and Strategy

Every business will face external changes and pressures from new competition, new regulatory rules, and new technologies—to name just a few— and a Smarts-oriented mind-set that complements strong Guts will facilitate decision making. It's easier to adjust strategy, or *pivot*, if you constantly feel out the pulse and voice of customers to assess their changing demand patterns. Ultimately, the customer should direct strategy, product development, and pricing choices. Pivoting is almost an expected part of the business-building journey in today's Internet and technology firms, with their iterative and flexible development methodologies and cultures. Leaders should communicate the reasons for shifts and pivots not as deviations from a larger strategy, but as adjustments based on clear facts and feedback. Soon they will be able to celebrate successes as customers gravitate toward those changes.

Crossroad: The Rich-Versus-King Dilemma

The Heart says one thing, while Smarts says another: does it make sense to "fire yourself"? Noam Wasserman, a professor of entrepreneurial management at Harvard Business School, describes a number of common scenarios he colloquially dubs the *rich-versus-king* dilemma. These range from seeking a cofounder (thus splitting the equity with a partner), to ceding control of a company to venture capitalists, to believing that a CEO who is not yourself might be able to increase your company's value. *King* options generally permit founders to keep control of key decisions and, often, to maintain more equity for themselves while possibly reducing the value of the company. *Rich* options enable the company—and the founder's stake—to potentially increase in value while the founder sacrifices control. The key here is recognizing that there is no single right answer. The rich-versus-king dilemma boils down to how well each choice matches a founder's motivation. The decision to take outside investment is another common trade-off. There are times when additional capital and experienced investors can clearly help a business create greater long-term value. Entrepreneurs who value control can sometimes make poor choices, whether it's refusing capital (and future growth) altogether, or holding out for whomever will give them the highest valuation and more control on their company, when in fact other capabilities may be required.

Crossroad: Knowing When to Change Your Founding Team Members

Blind loyalty is one of the main reasons businesses fail to scale. The Heart struggles with the human pull to remain faithful to the people who helped get us where we are today, while our Smarts tell us our businesses require a different course. To succeed, you have to be willing to subordinate yourself and your team members to the overall institutional purpose of the business you've created. Roles need to evolve alongside a company's growth, and blind fealty to colleagues can stanch that growth. We've known many leaders who have failed to recognize their cofounders' limitations by advancing them beyond their level of competence, just as we've known leaders who have failed to leverage the talents of their cofounders, thereby leading to discontent and an eventual exodus. Are your cofounders veering toward positive evolving roles or exiting ones?

Crossroad: Do I Keep or Sell My Business?

To be fair, this is a high-class problem, and a highly personal one. Some business-builders foresee an exit strategy from day one, while others enter business out of purer Heart- and purpose-driven passions (selling their businesses does not occur to them until much later). Selling is not binary. Per Noam Wasserman's rich-versus-king dilemma, it can mean taking any outside money as investment while building the business. But ultimately, the choice to sell a business and "cash out" is bittersweet. On one hand, it is a benchmark of success, with potentially meaningful financial rewards. On the other hand, entrepreneurs can feel as though they have sold their core meaning and purpose, and even betrayed their employees and customers. If you're facing this choice, ask yourself the diagnostic questions in "To Sell or Not to Sell?"

To Sell or Not to Sell?

Do you need to sell?

Build things with long-term value that have superior cash flow and you become in control of when to sell. A long-term, value-creating mind-set creates fewer exit-timing problems than an opportunistic, value-capture one. Put simply: build for value, not for sale.

Are you taking value-maximization too far?

Trying to time the peak perfectly is foolish. Too often people do not honestly assess the risk-adjusted trade-off between what will be required to get more value in the future versus what you can get today.

Can you take some chips off the table?

J.P. Morgan said, "I made all my money by selling too early."[9] If you can realize some liquidity, explore it seriously.

What is the market context?

If there are lots of buyers, it may be time to exit. But are you getting the best price? Ask if this is a buyer's or seller's market.

Do you *want* to sell?

Will you be happy selling? Or will you feel like you "sold out"? Are you confusing selling with wanting a different role? Separate your financial motivations from the nonfinancial reasons.

Recapping Crossroads and Thresholds of Guts-Dominant Individuals

Starting a business from scratch requires the courage to take risks despite possible, and even probable, negative consequences. Having the Guts to Initiate, to Endure, and to Evolve is essential to all stages of business-building. Ask any great business-builder, and he will tell you that the Guts to act at critical moments is the single most inspiring—and therefore memorable—element of his leadership. (That's *ex post facto*.) Before this breakthrough, however, many friends, family members, and colleagues doubtless told them they were absolutely out of their mind to think they could make their ideas work.

As we noted at the beginning of this chapter, the entrepreneurial and business-building journey can be a lonely one. If you are starting your own venture, or serving as the agent of change in a more mature business enterprise, we can promise that you will need to stand alone at times.

Successful companies are vigilant companies. They never rest. They never exhale. As a leader, the challenges you face may be different from those you've faced in the past, but they still require your attention. Even if you're on top of your industry, the willingness to *keep the fight going* is an admirable illustration of the Guts to Evolve. Where others might back down or become complacent, the gutsy entrepreneur will be on the lookout for ways to change, adapt, or secure new markets, while always anticipating competition anytime and anywhere.

The crossroads we have described in this chapter closely complement the key growth inflection points of a company's life cycle. Moving from the founding stage, to the proving stage, to scaling, and ultimately to the evolving and extending stages are all moments that require a founder to reexamine what the business requires. At each one of these stages, all business-builders require a threshold level of Guts. These are "mirror moments" in which you must ask yourself whether you are the right person to get the company to the next level, and what you need to change in yourself, and in the company, to make that happen. Are you going to retain the friend who has been with you from day one in X role, despite knowing he is no longer the right person for the job and, at minimum, needs to evolve to Y role? Are you willing to have that tough conversation? Are you willing to be objective, and do you have the right instincts to pinpoint the right time to double down instead of bailing out?

In short, "gutting it out" is a big part of any long-term business strategy.

Cutting across all the crossroads perhaps is the recurrent theme of how best to balance perseverance with flexibility. It is the business-builder's paradox. An ongoing delicate balance between: (1) having the relentless conviction and refusal of failure for one's vision and (2) embracing and dealing with failure when it inevitably comes. This leads to the perennial question asked by Guts-dominant people, "What do I stick to and what do I change?"

Countless successful entrepreneurs and experienced business-builders have given us their solution: remain constant with your core principles, and with everything else have courage to tweak, pivot, or change as the market dictates the need for such adjustments. Both sides of this equation—defining what needs to stay firm and constant versus what is open for change—demand Guts. The Guts to start something, stay with it, and ultimately evolve it is indeed the stuff great Gut-driven business-builders are made of.

CHAPTER IN SUMMARY

Guts: How to Initiate, Endure, and Evolve

- **What Guts Does:** Guts gives business-builders the courage to make things happen, stick with it, and remain confident against all odds.

- **Fear and Guts:** Guts-driven entrepreneurs aren't fearless; they just know how to cope with, and maybe even thrive in, uncomfortable environments.

- The Guts Hierarchy:

  - The Guts to Initiate: It takes Guts to start something. The Guts to Initiate empowers us to take a leap of faith despite an uncertain future.

  - The Guts to Endure: The Guts to Endure lets us recognize that failure is not an option but rather a reality. It's about remaining strong and resolute: persevering in the short-term to realize our longer-term goals.

  - The Guts to Evolve: A good business-builder has the self-awareness and readiness to pivot, evolve, or reset. The Guts to Evolve gives us the ability to enact change within ourselves, unleashing our inner potential to lead through natural business inflection points and thresholds.

- Guts Can Be Acquired: While some individuals are born with an innate level of Guts, it is indeed an acquirable trait. Early-life experiences, crisis training, and the right support network can all enhance our level of Guts.

- Four Common Crossroad Decisions That Require Guts: Guts-dominant individuals especially differentiate themselves during these challenging decision points.

  - Do I pivot and change the course of the business?

  - Do I replace myself as CEO?

  - Do I replace/change an early (or even founding) team member?

  - Do I sell?

  These business inflection points represent real "moments of truths" that test a leader's Guts.

- The Guts-Dominant Are Restless: Successful companies are vigilant, taking few breaks to rest or exhale. Inevitable trials and tribulations are part of the business-building growth cycle, and it is Guts more than any other trait that keeps the fight going and provides the courage to take action and adapt as necessary along the way.

- The Business-Builder's Paradox: Ultimately, the great paradox for the Guts-driven business-builder is the tightrope balance between refusing to accept failure and simultaneously embracing it when it appears. It is a perennial reflection on where to hold steadfast and where to adjust—an inner push-pull tension between conviction and humility. Awareness of this helps carry the day forward.

5

✦ *Luck's* INEVITABLE *Role* IN BUSINESS-BUILDING

There are no guarantees to entrepreneurial success. Your concept may be bold, your Heart quotient high, your Smarts and Guts peaking, but external factors beyond our control are always at play. The business environment is fickle, and business-builders can't ever fully predict where their concepts, or plans, will take them. Last-minute glitches or *UKVs*—unforeseen killer variables—are always lurking and threatening havoc, especially in early-stage businesses. A client may default, a promised source of funding may disappear, the world's markets may sour—any of these can shift your trajectory in an instant. Then again, you may be lucky. Your business idea may intersect with its time and culture as if it were meant to be.

Luck matters. Without it, Heart is a dream deferred, Smarts is just another bright or savvy person walking down the street, and Guts is scattershot intensity or stoic resilience waiting for something to tip. Whether it is serendipitous timing, a chance encounter, or a concept that ignites a deep need consumers never realized they had, Luck will always play a role in the business journey. While relatively few business-builders succeed solely on the basis of the Luck trait, there is no question in our minds that Luck is necessary. Frankly, it is the one quality of which we can never get enough.

The questions around the role that Luck plays remain: How to explain chance, good or bad? Can we harness it to influence us the way we'd like?

and, What is the optimal way to survive a period of *bad* Luck? In short, how do you create good Luck and embrace bad Luck?

By its classic definition, Luck is ungovernable. Luck has a mind of its own. Circumstances beyond our control will always occur—which is why acknowledging and understanding the role Luck plays in our business-building lives serves to remind us of our limitations. Success, money, and respect can lead to arrogance (just ask Icarus), so it is important to temper power with humility. And we've observed that humility and vulnerability, being open to new relationships, and appreciating that sometimes we just get a fortunate hand help us maintain conviction, courage, and momentum. And here's the thing: they also make us luckier.

Start looking into the career of any prominent business leader, and you'll find at least one story about the prominent role Luck played in his or her success or failure. Time and again in our interviews and research, some of the world's greatest entrepreneurs and business-builders spoke about Luck and their ability to create or influence it. A not-insignificant minority (more than one-fifth) of the hundreds of business creators and -builders we surveyed came out as Luck-dominant in their HSGL profile. In their business-building experiences, Luck was not completely beyond their control but something they could actually influence.

The secret? Luck is more about the right attitude and right relationships than anything else. Our conception of Luck is rooted in what we call a Lucky Attitude and a Lucky Network. The former is the result of humility, intellectual curiosity, and optimism. The latter is derived from the Lucky Attitude and adds such attributes as vulnerability, authenticity, generosity, and openness. One's Lucky Network represents the unpredictable, seemingly coincidental, and fortuitous relationships that help advance one forward.

In our E.A.T. survey research, we used trade-off question pairs, where survey participants were forced to choose between two personality traits. Figure 5-1 shows how Luck-dominant individuals answered certain options relative to their counterparts with different trait dominances. There are a few interesting elements to note. The first is the high percentage of Luck-dominant entrepreneurs who ascribe more of their success not to the more Guts-dominant traits of "doing things others feared or being resilient," but rather by "being open to trying new things" and "being in the right place at the right time." Whether through the survey or our interviews with business-builders, there is consistently an underlying humility and intellec-

Luck Defined

Luck \luhk\ *noun* 1 : right attitude intersecting with the right relationship network; the result of a Lucky Attitude (humility, intellectual curiosity, and optimism) and Lucky Network (subset of one's relationship network) composed of unexpected but highly useful relationships

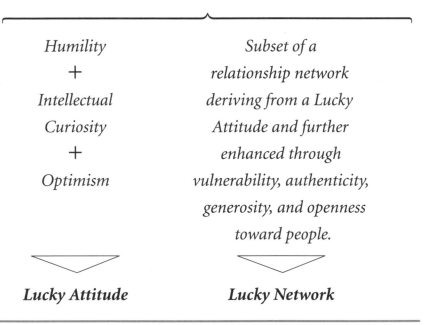

Humility
$+$
Intellectual Curiosity
$+$
Optimism

Lucky Attitude

Subset of a relationship network deriving from a Lucky Attitude and further enhanced through vulnerability, authenticity, generosity, and openness toward people.

Lucky Network

tual curiosity behind Luck-dominant people. In the trade-off question between whether persistence or optimism was more important, for example, it was optimism that resonated much more with the Luck-oriented. And finally, a further reflection of their humility and self-awareness is how they see their friends' perceptions of their success, noting that "friends would be more likely to say that I have been 'extremely fortunate' and 'luckier than most.'"

FIGURE 5-1

What Does It Mean to Be Luck-Driven?

PERCENT WHO CHOSE THE LUCK-ORIENTED RESPONSE

		LUCK-DOMINANT	ALL OTHERS
I'VE BEEN SUCCESSFUL THANKS TO:			
Doing things that others feared ←······>	Being open to trying new things	86%	64%
Being resilient ←······>	Being in the right place at the right time	57%	12%
WHICH STATEMENT RESONATES MORE?			
At work, I am more excited than most ←······>	At work, I am luckier than most	39%	9%
I am persistent ←······>	I am optimistic	75%	31%
MY FRIENDS WOULD BE MORE LIKELY TO SAY THAT:			
I have succeeded against all odds ←······>	I have been extremely fortunate	71%	48%
If I fail, it won't be for lack of intellectual horsepower ←······>	I am luckier than most	64%	32%

Defining a Lucky Attitude

Some people believe in Luck—and this belief makes them luckier. Luck is part of their optimistic outlook and openness to new things. They embrace the notion that there are other forces beyond themselves and their own understanding as well as serendipitous encounters that play a critical role to their success.

There are many things that make up this Lucky Attitude, but most important is the trifecta of humility, intellectual curiosity, and optimism. We will dig deeper into each of these three elements later in the chapter, but for now here's a brief definition of the three most important factors toward creating your own Luck.

- The foundation of a Lucky Attitude is *humility*. Management researcher Jim Collins, author of *Good to Great*, was among the first to note humility as a key trait of high-performing leaders.[1] Having what we dub a Lucky Attitude begins with awareness of your own limitations; appreciation of the broader efforts of those around you; and a nonjudgmental stance. If you're in a position of power and leadership this is not always easy. You need enough self-confidence to win the respect of others, but that confidence (which often comes with positional authority) needs to be counterbalanced with the recognition that there is so much more you don't know. Humility humanizes leaders and permits them to be luckier. It is the root of self-awareness, and it creates the space to take on our next Lucky Attitude trait: intellectual curiosity.

- *Intellectual curiosity* is an active response to humility. Humility leads to intellectual curiosity or at least the capacity for it. Think about it. People who are fully confident or even arrogant are less likely to question their personal assumptions or outlook on the world. A business-builder who is intellectually curious has a voracious desire to learn more about just about anything. He devours books, listens to suggestions, and tirelessly explores new ideas. In the end, thanks to his willingness to meet new people, ask new questions, and go to new places, he has a greater chance of being exposed to and rewarded by Luck.

- *Optimism* is the energy source for positive change. If humility is the foundation for intellectual curiosity, then optimism gives people the belief, inspiration, and energy that enable the realization of new possibilities. More, better, and faster is always possible in the mind-set of an optimist. It is a self-fulfilling prophecy: more Luck tends to come to those people who believe in possibility and see the good in something before they see the bad. Optimists are givers of energy rather than takers of it. Their positive dispositions put them in the path of a greater number of "surprise" encounters with good fortune. Driven by an unshakable belief in the potential for better, they tend as well to act on what they find through their intellectually curious pursuits. This completes the virtuous circle of the Lucky Attitude: optimism coupled with execution capabilities is what allows us to take full advantage of the Luck bestowed on us.

The luckiest people in the business world are those who say to themselves: I am humble enough to realize I don't know how to and can't do most things on my own; I am curious and courageous enough to ask questions that might be embarrassingly naive; and I embrace the "glass half-full" optimism that the end result can always be improved on.

Defining a Lucky Network

Once you have that Lucky Attitude, you can start building a Lucky Network. In today's socially connected, LinkedIn, and Facebooked world, the notion that one's relationship network is the product of serendipity can feel silly. But it is absolutely clear to us that a Lucky Network is the product of art as well as science.

On the science side, there are clear processes and best practices that can help one improve the size and quality of one's relationship network, from the popular social networking sites mentioned and others, to appropriately managing and tagging one's database of contacts, to some of the Smarts Habits we describe in our People Smarts section in chapter 3 (e.g., triaging your most impactful relationships). It only takes an armchair statistician to point out that the more people in whose path you have placed yourself, the more opportunities will come your way. But the Lucky Network side of relationship development, the artful aspect of this dance, is a little more interesting. Who are those people in your network who want to share their paths with you? When it comes to relationships, Tsun-yan notes, the power of pull is greater than that of push.

The Lucky Network is the slice of one's relationship network that seems more serendipitous, less predictable, and more orthogonal than the science side. The NPV—net present value—and strategic fit of a given relationship in one's Lucky Network might be foggy at best, but that's the point. You can't always predict which relationships will be important to you later. We have all seen or experienced when some random acquaintance can suddenly be of great value. A sister of a high school friend becomes a critical first employee; a former colleague of a colleague from another country becomes a senior executive at a big technology company where you are trying to get an "in"; a guy working in a paint store learns to code, happens to be damned good at it, and ends up as one of your lead engineers (these are all real examples, by the way).

To drive the point further, consider some fictional examples. In the movie *Slumdog Millionaire*, the protagonist is able to win a television game show because of a series of seemingly unlinked yet, in the end, crucial relationship encounters. In *Forrest Gump*, the hero's unlikely friendship with Lieutenant Dan leads to the formation of the Bubba Gump Shrimp Company and then Dan's decision to invest the profits in Apple Computer shares. (Wonder if they still own the stock now?)

The art and Luck side of a relationship network, we will see, arises from the three primary Lucky Attitude elements but also the secondary relationship building characteristics of vulnerability, generosity, authenticity, and openness. The Lucky Network brings together a set of relationships that play critical roles at the right time but that could not have been a priori predicted to do so. The benefit of having a Lucky Network is that it is a wild card that will bring about unpredictable but positive impact to your business endeavors and your life in general.

We'll get into more depth on both Lucky Attitude and Lucky Network later in this chapter, but first let's shift gears for a moment to examine the different kinds of Luck.

Types of Luck

Luck comes in three forms: Dumb Luck, Constitutional Luck, and Circumstantial Luck. Of these, it is Circumstantial Luck that we can influence the most. Constitutional Luck deals with elements and environments into which you are born, and Dumb Luck is just what it sounds like—and is therefore least within our sphere of influence potential.

Dumb Luck

When we pick a card from a deck, we have a roughly 2 percent chance of drawing the ace of hearts. In short, the odds that that card will end up in our hands are slight, but a small chance exists that it might. Unless we've rigged the deck in advance, we have no control whatsoever over the outcome. Whatever card we end up holding will simply have to do with neutral probability, or put another way, pure Dumb Luck.

In some cases—think card counters playing blackjack—it's possible to manage what appears to be Dumb Luck through statistical and analytical means. This amounts to transforming Dumb Luck into Smarts. But real Dumb Luck can't be managed away like that, and sometimes the people who win the biggest jackpots are those who are most oblivious to the risks. A person may have bet a few bucks on horse number 22 without realizing that while he intended to bet $7.00 he bet $700 by accident. Oops. His horse wins—and so does he. It's doubtful he would have taken the chance or risk had he known how much money was at stake. Because we cannot govern this kind of Dumb Luck, we won't say much about it here.

Constitutional Luck

We are each born with a certain makeup into a specific environment. We could be born in a new, fast-growing economy like Brazil or China, or in an Old World city, or some small town. We could be the products of an immigrant family, of parents who expected a little or a lot, from a privileged background with money or its absence. Heritage, gender, cultural background, family values, and upbringing predispose us to certain opportunities and future outcomes.

Many years ago, when Tsun-yan was a young, inexperienced consultant, a top senior executive took a distinct liking to him simply because he felt a connection with Hsieh's Chinese background. In the occasionally closed world of business, the Luck of a certain cultural or hereditary background can be a positive factor (though we've noticed it can backfire, too). In Tsun-yan's case, his Constitutional Luck—the Luck he was born with—worked in his favor.

Age and the era in which you were born can influence Luck, too. Many well-known entrepreneurs graduated college and began their professional careers during the birth of the commercial Internet. This timing proved exceptionally lucky for Tony. Not only was he able to learn countless lessons founding and building a leading Internet company in the early years of the Web's commercialization, but other opportunities popped up as well. At a relatively young age, he was given the chance to meet several *Fortune* 500 executives because these older executives were struggling to understand the impact of the Internet. He made an angel investment in a very young Internet company that in less than a year sold for nearly $1 billion. To be sure, other HSGL elements played a big role, too, but the Constitutional Luck of good timing was clearly one of the most critical factors benefiting him.

Warren Buffett has famously credited most of his success to Luck. He claims he won the "ovarian lottery" by being born at the right time in a country where his skill set of being wired for capital markets and being able to allocate capital could amass great wealth.[2] It is a humbling insight into an amazing success story. Buffett uses the ovarian lottery analogy to ask people to imagine that there is a ball representing each person on the earth. He jokes that if he was one of those balls pulled out during a different era, say millions of years ago, he'd be pretty useless and likely eaten by some dinosaur. In a similar fashion, he acknowledges that his gift of allocating capital is driven by the circumstances of where he is—if he were on a desert island without a capital market, the value of his skill goes nearly to zero. Buffett calculates that when he was born, he had a roughly one-in-fifty chance of being in a situation where his particular skills were valuable. Had he been born to different family circumstances, in a different era, or in another country where there were fewer opportunities for investors, he would never have had the opportunity to become the success he is today.

Since our nature and nurture define our Constitutional Luck, we cannot adjust or reinvent it. We can, however, decide whether to take advantage of it. It is up to each of us to see how our Constitutional Luck can be leveraged and maximized. Reflecting on and understanding how to use your constitutional elements as *Luck levers* is an exercise always worth doing. For most of the readers of this book, you will find that if you think about it, you are already born into one of the luckiest situations available on the planet.

Circumstantial Luck

You're planning to meet your older brother for a casual lunch at a new restaurant. At the last minute, he calls to say he's running late. It's a warm, sunny afternoon and, as you make your way into a nearby park, you catch sight of an old friend you haven't seen in years. After enthusiastically telling her about your new business, your old friend suggests you speak with an acquaintance of hers who, twelve months later, will step up to become your company's CEO and drive it to new levels of success.

If your brother had been punctual; if you hadn't then gone to kill time at the park; if you hadn't spotted your old friend; if the two of you hadn't reunited; if you hadn't gone into detail about your business; if she hadn't recommended her friend as a trustworthy resource—then your business's profit may never have increased tenfold under an outstanding new CEO. You were uncannily lucky in the course of events, a category of fortune we dub Circumstantial Luck. This type of Circumstantial Luck epitomizes how apparently small and trivial events can have disproportionately influential consequences. Run into enough trivial events and eventually, one or two may turn out to be large and meaningful. (So long as you are willing to act on the luck presented to you.)

Timing is everything, and you can't time anything.

We often dub being at the right place at the right time an accident, a coincidence, or even fate. But it is possible to influence Circumstantial Luck. "Timing is everything, and you can't time anything," notes entrepreneur Kimbal Musk.[3] "So just try and be in as many places as you can at the right time."

Circumstantial Luck is arguably responsible for the creation of Red Bull, the now ubiquitous energy drink found across college libraries during finals period and at extreme sports events around the world. It was created in 1987 when Dietrich Mateschitz, an Austrian who was in Thailand working for a German toothpaste company, noticed that the locals were extremely enthusiastic about a drink called Krating Daeng (Thai for "water buffalo"). His curiosity piqued, Mateschitz decided to try this "liquid water buffalo." The energy drink cured his jet lag, and he understood why Thai truck drivers were such fans. Seeing potential, he had the insight to carbonate the drink and sell it in the West. Red Bull shipped over 4 billion cans in 2010.

How does one business-builder get to be Luckier than another? Chances are that the people we perceive as fortunate are consciously or subconsciously following the principles of a Lucky Attitude and a Lucky Network. They are humble. They are intellectually curious. They are optimistic. And they also tend to develop pretty great relationship networks, not so much by trying hard as by naturally, authentically, and generously giving and caring about people.

Why (and How) Ignorance Can Matter Toward Luck

Experience has shown us two types of successful entrepreneurs who benefit from a strange variant of Circumstantial Luck. The first group is made up of men and women who, by embracing constraints, in turn become more creative. People can become more creative, and almost by definition need to be, when limitations are put on them. The members of the second group, whom we highlight in this section, are oblivious to such limitations—whether they exist in reality or not. They freely generate ideas because ignorance is their friend. Having an optimistic, Forrest Gump–like view on the world can unlock new perspectives. If you are oblivious to, or dismissive of, the risk factors in a given business situation, you might ultimately end up becoming more successful. It's curious when you think about it: knowing your constraints in one case helps drive creativity, but not knowing them can also drive you toward innovative brilliance.

What do we think about this? Well, if necessity is the mother of innovation, this innocent variety of ignorance—we're not talking about willful stupidity here—may be the father. We say this for two reasons. First, ignorance can mean having an open mind that is free from constraints; and second, ignorance can increase your convictions and your fearlessness. If you are oblivious to the risks involved in a given situation, your apprehension about succeeding or not succeeding will fall accordingly. It is hard to be afraid of what you don't know.

Which is why in a company's early stages, a blindness to external influences can stimulate both creativity and innovation (after all, we seldom lose sleep over risks we know nothing about). For the very same reasons, many strikingly bold insights come from younger people. Youth is not burdened with the experience to prejudice new ways of thinking. Experience and wisdom may be necessary to grow and sustain a company, but naiveté and disruptive thinking both go a long way toward generating ceiling-busting ideas and behaviors. Thus, within the context of entrepreneurship and idea generation, ignorance—again, the good kind—can create an inspiring environment of open-mindedness and innovation. It doesn't hurt to recognize those critical moments in a company's trajectory—among others, the conceptualization phase and certain growth inflection points—when a clean-sheet approach is a net positive.

A Zen master may have put it best. In his book, *Zen Mind, Beginner's Mind*, Shunryū Suzuki argues that an unfixed mind free of biases, preconceptions, judgments, criticisms, and expectations is therefore alive and awake to wonder, observe, process, and innovate.[4] By combining *knowing* and *not knowing*, the brain enables creativity and conviction—two essential entrepreneurial traits—to thrive. The former is most critical during a company's early, think-big stages, whereas the latter is vital to mobilizing your team to execute with continual excellence. "In the beginner's mind there are many possibilities," Suzuki was quoted once as saying. "In the expert's mind there are few."

Dumb Luck: Even a broken clock is right twice a day.

Developing a Lucky Attitude

The point of this chapter is that there are things you can do to increase your Luck. That's what the Lucky Attitude and Lucky Network are about. That seemingly innate ability that some people have to catch the perfect wave as it crests is at least in part a skill that can be developed. So let us go into more depth on, first, the Lucky Attitude.

Humility

Luck is about the fine line between control and out of control, about acknowledging where your control ends and the rest of the world begins. Anyone who claims he succeeded solely by his own effort is kidding himself. That's where humility comes in.

In our talks with hundreds of entrepreneurs and business leaders for this project, plus meeting hundreds more over the course of our careers, we've noticed one outstanding thing: a disproportionately high number of successful business-builders are humble—about what they know and don't know, about their own developmental needs, and about the team members they'll need to get the job done—for this trait not to be important. It is the opposite of overconfidence, whose hallmark brazenness may lead to grand visions but ultimately lackluster results.

If it weren't for his humility, the great anthropologist Clifford Geertz would not have made some of his most important contributions to the field. When he went to Bali in the 1970s, the locals didn't respond to his inquiries. They saw him and his wife as outsiders. So he worked hard to integrate himself with the locals by having the humility and respect to follow their customs and norms. When police arrived to break up an illegal cockfight that they were watching with a group of Balinese men, Geertz and his wife ran and hid with the locals until the scene cleared. The Balinese teased Geertz and his wife—they were white foreigners, and needn't have feared arrest—but also began to trust and respect them.

Humility in leadership starts with understanding that the purpose behind a vision goes beyond any one individual, and then realizing that achieving the vision will require ideas, resources, and new skills beyond what you have today. There is often an underlying quiet confidence in those who display humility, and a loud insecurity in those who display arrogance. Humble people are rewarded with more Luck, as they are quicker to explore new methods and ideas (the intellectual curiosity we will discuss next) and they are also quicker to share credit and recognition with others, yielding greater loyalty and respect. Luck comes more often to the person who seeks to earn respect than to the person who commands it through positional authority.

Intellectual Curiosity

Fact: If you focus continually on improving yourself, you will create more, and luckier, opportunities. Business leaders who make it a habit to question the norm and seek to better themselves and their businesses tend to end up lucky. Why? They're eager to read new things, reframe ideas, seek external input, sample new experiences, and exploit the boundaries of their own curiosity—all of which increase the likelihood of greater Circumstantial Luck coming their way. This may sound like hard work or discipline, but it has more to do with an individual's inner resolve to learn and an openness to the power of self-improvement. *There is always more to see and more to learn* is a great mantra for intercepting and even summoning Luck. Without humility and vulnerability, we can never possess the intellectual curiosity that a great leader requires.

One key is being willing to learn from anyone. When we asked Joe Grano, who was formerly CEO of UBS PaineWebber and now runs the investment firm Centurion Holdings, who inspires him, Joe answered, "To be honest, almost everyone inspires me. I have just as much fun talking to the gardener as I do talking to other CEOs. I've never met anyone whom I couldn't learn from, and when I approach relationships with that mind-set, they are always inspirational."[5] The data from our E.A.T. survey research reflected this attitude among Luck-dominant individuals. They tend to draw their influences from many different sources, whereas other entrepreneurs we observed tended to be influenced by mostly family or professional relationships (see figure 5-2). The larger the bubble, the heavier the influence from that source. Note how for Luck-driven business builders the bubbles are much more evenly distributed. This reflects a tendency to learn, as Joe Grano noted, "from everyone."

> Luck-dominant individuals are more equally distributed in where they draw their influence, learning from everyone.

Closely related to intellectual curiosity is a skill we borrow from Smarts: observing patterns. Some variants of Luck come down to recognizing a pattern where others see only a random series of events, trends, or behaviors. Observing doesn't necessarily mean absorbing more information. It's more a matter of combining information from the world around you with

FIGURE 5-2

Sources of Influence by HSGL Dominance

AVERAGE PERCENT ASSIGNED TO EACH INFLUENCE SOURCE

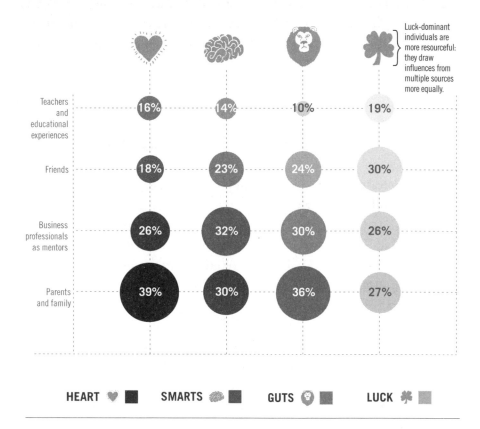

other, seemingly unrelated bits of pop culture, your own experiences, and Guts, and the behaviors of those around you. Pattern recognition can come together to propel one decision over another, as those who read chapter 3 already know.

At the Thomson Corporation, the decision to divest the core newspaper business came from Dick's being curious enough to observe the trends taking place around him. We were aware of a transition going on. He took note of the growing power of the Internet and how it shifted patterns in advertising. Ultimately, he concluded that the Web would seriously jeopardize newspapers—this was in the late 1990s. Some Smarts, some Guts, and the attendant intellectual curiosity of a Lucky Attitude led him to get out when he did.

In short, the need to be highly observant of the changes going on around you and the willingness to act on those changes are essential. What often comes across as "good" or "lucky" timing has as much to do with maintaining a generously observant mind-set.

Optimism

It turns out that feeling lucky and optimistic can grant confidence, improve performance, and push us to aim higher. Feeling lucky and optimistic allows us to release nervous tension and gives us the illusion of control in a seemingly random universe.

Michael Jordan wore his signature blue underwear in the name of good luck; Tiger Woods made red-shirt Sunday a symbolic ritual.[6] Alan Hassenfeld, former chairman of Hasbro, has told the story of putting seven lucky pennies in his shoe prior to a critical shareholder meeting.[7] Can good-luck charms literally heighten performance?

Yes. In one experiment, social psychologists Lysann Damisch, Barbara Stoberock, and Thomas Mussweiler from the University of Cologne gave twenty-eight golfers a ball branded as "lucky." Ultimately, these study subjects made, on average, 33 percent more winning putts than the rest of the group, who played with a "normal" ball.[8] There is a Luck-placebo effect when people believe they are receiving or are more predisposed to good fortune. Additional experiments assessed the effects of participants' lucky charms on both memory and puzzle solving. Again, in the presence of their talismans, subjects performed better. Researchers theorized that activating a superstition and/or positive mind-set led to higher self-set goals, as well as greater persistence in the performance of the task.

With or without good-luck charms, optimists experience better Luck in many aspects of their lives. Psychologists Christopher Peterson, George Vaillant, and Martin Seligman define a *pessimistic explanatory style* as one that perceives bad occurrences as global (e.g., affecting many areas of an individual's life), unlikely to change, and personal. In contrast, an *optimistic explanatory style* perceives bad events as insubstantial, short-lived, more likely than not to right themselves, and beyond any one person's control.

They found that optimistic college freshmen tended to attain higher GPAs in their first year of college (they are less likely to allow one bad grade to knock them off-course).[9]

Optimism can even prolong an individual's life. Using responses to questionnaires on wartime experiences, the same research team rated ninety-nine men on their explanatory style. After assessing their subjects' physical health over thirty-five years, the team found clear correlations between optimism and physical and even mental condition. It seems optimists are determined to improve their health and they take better care of themselves. Moreover, they generally boast stronger support networks of family and friends.[10]

Tony Hsieh of Zappos told us about an intriguing experiment conducted by British psychologist Richard Wiseman. In 2003, Wiseman assembled a group divided evenly between those who described themselves as "lucky" and those who described themselves as "unlucky." Next, Wiseman tasked his study subjects to leaf through a newspaper. Those who calculated the correct number of photographs inside would be awarded $100. On the second page, Wiseman included this bold, two-inch-high message: STOP COUNTING—THERE ARE 43 PHOTOGRAPHS IN THIS NEWSPAPER.

The lucky study subjects were much more likely to notice this message than the unlucky ones, and were able to complete the task ten times faster. By being attentive and observant, the lucky people were able to seize the chance to sidestep unnecessary counting and go on to happily collect their $100 prize.[11]

From additional personality tests, Wiseman also discovered that his lucky study subjects were plagued by far less anxiety than the unlucky subjects, confirming previous studies that have shown that anxiety about one particular activity impedes our ability to observe elements of our peripheral environment.

Pessimists focus on what could have been better, while optimists focus what could have been worse. What we often brush away as Luck is, in fact, a mind-set of openness, readiness, and optimism.

While this mind-set is to some extent congenital, you can work to develop it. Here's a practical tool to combat the cynic in us all: the 24 × 3 rule. The next time you hear a new idea, wait twenty-four seconds before saying or thinking something negative. This reinforces a foundational skill of

Jay Chiat on Leading with Optimism

Tony Tjan has had some incredible mentors. One was the advertising genius Jay Chiat. Jay thought differently and decidedly optimistically. After Converse secured the official 1984 Olympic sponsorship, Jay painted Los Angeles (literally) with Nike murals. The public assumed that Jay's client, Nike, and not Converse, was the games' official sponsor.[12] Jay bequeathed Tony two lifelong lessons:

- Embrace constraints as a source of creativity: Great entrepreneurs seldom complain about what they lack, but focus instead on what they have, and what they can do with it. The same goes for leaders.

- Focus on the positive before the negative: Mavericks and entrepreneurs stress optimism before pessimism. When someone pitches you an idea, stop. Before your mind leaps to the negatives, focus on the reasons this idea might succeed. The enduring lesson: lead with optimism.

optimists and leaders: listening. As you gain the ability to pause for twenty-four seconds before letting the critic in you bubble to the surface, move to the next level and try twenty-four minutes. At twenty-four minutes, you can give more considered thought to why it might actually work and why it might just topple conventional wisdom.

And yes, you should work toward waiting twenty-four hours—one whole day—before verbalizing the cons against something. Most times this will not be possible. Our minds cannot compartmentalize so easily. But the 24 × 3 rule is a type of reflective meditation for developing a more optimistic approach toward people and ideas.

Developing a Lucky Network

A Lucky Network is key to understanding the overall Luck equation. Standing there as a sometimes inscrutable collaborator to the Lucky Attitude, a

Lucky Network represents the wallflowers, the ringers, the unsung heroes of your Rolodex. There are deliberate, strategic, and methodological ways to build a strong network. A Lucky Network is not that. It is instead that curious cross-section of your contacts that an outside eye might find surprising and even out of place in terms of potential impact and relevance. Members of this subset might not be famous or powerful; they might not be in your industry; they probably hold little apparent strategic value. What stands out about this network is that the relationships are authentic and generous. They are the relationships in which you are most willing to show vulnerability and openness, deeper relationships that over the long run intersect in direct and indirect ways with your business life.

The relationships within a Lucky Network are intrinsically rewarding. They are not overly-calculated or strategic but rather are friends and acquaintances who bring diversity, openness, and a genuine interest in your success, independent of a business objective. These people may include an old friend, a mentor, a mentee, a partner, a spouse, or acquaintances in the arts and academia. Bottom line: it could be anyone, but it is the nature of your relationship with these people that is different from just another contact. If one were to consider a personal relationship map that had two axes—on its Y-axis is relevance/impact to business and on its X-axis is depth of relationship—the Lucky Network members are more likely to be the people to the right side of the X-axis and relatively low on the Y-axis of current business relevance/impact.

So how does a Lucky Network help? For right now, it is the support that members of the Lucky Network often provide that is most valuable. But there is also a latent long-term potential for more direct business relevance. You can also explain the value of a Lucky Network with simple logic. If your network is just like everyone else's in your field, you will probably end up in the same paths as your peers. If your network is markedly different, has quirky sets of folks here and there, then there is a good chance you'll end up different, too. For many of the Luck-dominant, this ragtag bucket of contacts tends to produce incredible opportunities over time—opportunities that no one, even the Luck-dominant, could have predicted.

A Lucky Network is built not around social aspirations, but on a genuine interest in other people. Here is a simple example to which most can relate. Mentoring provides present-day psychic reward, but usually not much in the way of tangible short-term return on investment. People can be successful in business without doing much of it. But over the long run, someone who has mentored a group of high-potential stars will have developed valuable business relationships with deep and genuine histories. This has been true in spades for Tsun-yan and his long list of mentees-turned-peers and -leaders across different organizations.

This Lucky Network is in part the product of a Lucky Attitude—that magic combination of humility, intellectual curiosity, and optimism. But there are four related attitudinal traits that can further enhance its development. Seven is a lucky number, and there are just that many character traits positively reinforcing to one another in a Lucky Network: humility, intellectual curiosity, optimism, vulnerability, authenticity, generosity, and openness. As with the Ten Commandments, it is not necessarily easy to recall all of these, or to separate out their nuances. But when you contemplate them, they are almost unassailable in terms of an ideal. Few will have even a majority of these attributes as part of their natural style, but increasing returns to a Lucky Network come to those who learn to manifest more of them.

Humility. Humility helps business leaders realize their own shortcomings and dependency on others (both on their team and beyond) to accomplish a vision. Humble leaders are thus predisposed to taking a general interest in other people. Where an arrogant business-builder may look down on others, the humble leader looks at others with interest and even admiration. As Dale Carnegie once wrote, "You can make more friends in two months by becoming interested in other people than you can in two years by trying to get other people interested in you."[13] Have the humility to show interest in more people—and watch as more Circumstantial Luck comes your way. People with humility tend to be liked—go figure—and contacts in one's Lucky Network will be more likely to want to introduce interesting opportunities, offer help, and share experiences with you.

Intellectual Curiosity. Intellectual curiosity extends a general interest in others from a purely utilitarian position to one of deep-rooted passion and interest in new people. Exit interviews from Richard Wiseman's experiment on counting photos in newspapers also revealed that many of the "lucky" subjects actively embraced novelty and variety in their lives. They had an intellectual curiosity toward meeting new people. To counteract his tendency to talk to the same type of person at parties, one such person told Wiseman he spoke only to people wearing a particular color. A genuine curiosity about different people propelled him to make new relationships outside of his usual peer group, allowing him to explore new prospects.

Intellectual curiosity is also what enabled Alan Zafran, cofounder and partner at Luminous Capital, an investment adviser that oversees almost $5 billion in client assets, to take advantage of some Circumstantial Luck that set in motion his investment career.

Zafran recalled being an undergrad on a rainy night on the Stanford campus, where he worked in the career office but didn't have much of a career plan himself. "I was hungry and didn't want to ride my bike back in the rain to my fraternity house to get food, so I crashed an MBA cocktail information hour next door."[14] Despite knowing little about the technical aspects of corporate finance, Zafran had long been fascinated by the Wall Street cognoscenti: What made these people tick? Why did they do the deals they did? How did they get to where they are today? And this curiosity paid off when Zafran successfully winged his way through a spontaneous conversation with a senior banker at the cocktail hour. Impressed, the banker invited Zafran to New York, where he did much better at asking questions than answering them and was offered a job that would lead him on a path from Goldman Sachs to Merrill Lynch to Luminous Capital, where he would make the prescient—we won't call it Lucky—decision to bet against subprime mortgages.

Optimism. Optimism enables people to view others as sources of energy and to be givers of positive energy. Their thirst for learning, encouragement of others, and overall positivity has a magnifying and multiplying effect. Their view on the ability to do better and bigger things inspired them and their optimistic belief in people and the capacity for people to achieve those things rallies and inspires others. It is optimism and the ability to project that helps one expand his Lucky Network across a broader group.

We have all been in the presence of takers of energy. These are the natural critics who are the quickest to give a comment on why something won't work. Do you enjoy hanging out with people like that? Believers in possibility tend to be surrounded by more interesting people. Whom do you know who has the most interesting set of authentic relationships? How much of an optimist is he?

Vulnerability. Vulnerability, like humility, is based on the precept that one does not know everything. Particularly important is *active vulnerability*—putting yourself out there to take a risk that might make you look foolish if it fails. This is where vulnerability goes beyond humility. You can be humble by not boasting of your accomplishments and giving thanks and credit to others, but vulnerability is about actively acknowledging areas of weakness and taking risks into new frontiers. This may feel like hairsplitting, but the nuance is important because both humility and vulnerability represent areas of improvement for many business-builders. Think of the business leaders with whom you have worked. How many have openly shared with you their weaknesses, their development needs? Do they embrace the tools of a 360 review and open dialogue with colleagues, or do they view those things as painful requirements? Vulnerability yields a higher quality of a Lucky Network *pulling* people to you. When a leader is vulnerable, the troops often work even harder because people want to help where they feel their help has impact. Humility and vulnerability are about realizing the need for help, with the latter amounting to an implicit request for it.

Authenticity. Authenticity has come up before. It was the secret sauce to the nuance of the Heart, for which an authentic vision and passion are key. Authenticity is explained well by the famous last piece of advice Polonius offered Laertes in Hamlet: "To thine own self be true." There is a reason this quotation is so frequently repeated. It is a good one!

Here we take it to mean that your dealings, conversations, and actions with your Lucky Network are true expressions of your interests and feelings. Tsun-yan frames this state as the *congruent self*. In other words, I say what I think, what I think is how I feel, and how I feel is who I am. Pause and read that again. Are you really interested in the family history of the budding musician? In the meandering and philosophical thoughts of a friendly policy wonk? Or in the trials and tribulations of an academic experimenter? Lucky people are. Don't pretend to be in the hopes of backing into Luck. You can't reverse engineer it. Feigned interest, whether it stems from benevolent obsequiousness or less honorable manipulation, will not help your Lucky Network flourish. An authentic relationship with a Lucky contact will do more for your happiness and chance of success than a forced relationship with someone you think is powerful or important.

Generosity. Generosity is asking not what you can get out of a new relationship but how you can help the person. Helping five new people will probably prove much more useful to you in the course of your career than trying to extract quick favors from five new contacts. When you discover and connect with great people who might be off of the radar, don't just meet them—take to heart Keith Ferrazzi's precept of leading with generosity.[15] Lucky Networks are strengthened by bets on good people, whether it is your time to offer some advice or perhaps make a helpful introduction. At the very least, you will feel good about offering a hand— it is better to give than to receive when you have someone worthwhile to give to.

Openness. Openness, in the eyes of the lucky, is about welcoming things that might not fit a traditional mold. A simple example is how the lucky people receive intelligence and wisdom from all sources in an effort to further their view of the world. Do you only give credence to facts if they are in the *New York Times,* or do you listen to people whose positional power may be low but whose real-world experience is high? The open source software phenomenon, and crowdsourcing more broadly, was built on this notion—that insights and good work can come from anywhere. We are not suggesting that every decision be put to the masses for a vote, but it only makes sense to consult a wider pool than oneself.

Whether collective wisdom from an advisory group, the collective viewpoint of customers, or the collective opinion of one's employees, the art of listening and taking input from others is a skill we can always improve.

The Luck-dominant are also open enough to avoid the trap of relative evaluation, which economist Dan Ariely describes as judging someone based not on a global set of people but against their micro-contextualized peers.[16] For example, an MBA student may fall short of his peers on financial acumen, but when compared with them on a broader basis, he may stand out for his dogged work ethic, positive attitude, and insatiable curiosity. How lucky to have a chance to meet him. While it's sometimes efficient to stick to certain molds and forms, Lucky people are open enough to sense when such rigidity is missing the bigger picture.

Ultimately, openness is about pushing leaders to think less of themselves as the best athlete than being the best person to create a great team and realize its collective potential.

Lucky Attitude, Lucky Network

"Luck," Tsun-yan says, "is that factor that explains a business outcome above and beyond that which can be reasonably expected." Uncertainty can provide something above and beyond expectations, but "uncertainty has to collide with something else to provide a Lucky outcome." That something is the Lucky Network. What are networks anyway but structures, or fishnets, that we cast to catch relationships that open wide the door to a universe of shifting variables? Random events from that network will undoubtedly spill over in positive ways in your own life.

But again, Luck does not simply find you. You need a Lucky Attitude, and a Lucky Network, to catch it.

When Bad Luck Calls

Just as we have moments and periods of "wave-surfing," when just about anything we touch goes our way and when we are on the crest, we often face periods when life is a welter of mistakes, dashed opportunities, and rugs yanked out from under us. Even if a team performs exceptionally well, outside factors might conspire against it—a major new competitive entrant, an unanticipated change in the regulatory environment, a terrorist attack, and so on. Failure does not necessarily reflect poorly on you as a person. Just as hard work and Smarts do not necessarily lead to success, bad Luck happens. It's how you deal with it can distinguish you.

In one context or another, you've likely failed. You may have framed it in terms less harsh than outright *failure*, but if you look honestly in the mirror, you can almost certainly point to at least one or two significant business missteps. First, congratulations, and welcome to the club. You are normal. We've all been there. Second, unless your failure involved a capital crime, you now have the opportunity to learn from your mistake, recover, and improve your approach to the next challenge. In this section, we offer a story of failure ("Tony Tjan on the IPO That Got Away") and a checklist for dealing with failure ("Our Five Questions to Help Overcome 'Failure'").

Tony Tjan on the IPO That Got Away

In the mid-1990s, along with a former McKinsey colleague and several business school classmates, I founded ZEFER, one of the first Internet strategy and development firms in the United States. Back then, companies were just awakening to the commercial opportunities of the Web, and our timing couldn't have been better. Thanks to ZEFER's interdisciplinary approach across business, design, and technology, we were poised to take advantage of one of the most spectacular aberrations in business history.

By early 2000, ZEFER had grown to nine hundred people, raised tens of millions of dollars, and boasted annual revenue on pace for more than $100 million. Big global clients like Thomson, McKinsey, Morgan Stanley, Siemens, and others had engaged us to develop and implement their Internet strategies.

We were an industry darling, and we decided to go public.

After intense months of preparing the regulatory filings and other work that a public offering requires, in the spring of 2000 we readied ourselves for our IPO roadshow (the process of pitching our stock to prospective investors). During a grueling two-week stretch, a cadre of bankers shepherded our management team through more than eighty back-to-back meetings across the United States and Europe. The process reminded me of the film *Groundhog Day*, but adrenaline and continued interest in our stock kept us going through fifteen- to eighteen-hour days.

This time around, though, our timing couldn't have been worse. Our IPO was scheduled for April 14, 2000—about a month after the great Internet stock bubble had begun to deflate. On April 13, I was in New York twenty-four hours before what was intended to be a ceremonial, celebratory visit to NASDAQ to launch our IPO. It didn't happen. The exchange had lost about 35 percent of its value in three weeks. We decided that we had to withdraw our stock offering. The irrational exuberance of the dot-com boom shifted overnight to a dot-com bust. It was the onset of a nuclear winter for Internet businesses.

We'd put our hearts and souls into the company. Our rise had been fast and ferocious. But soon we would need to face the reality not just of the IPO that got away, but also of downsizing the company and laying off employees who had become close friends and collaborators.

At the time, ZEFER's missed IPO—and from such a pinnacle, too—felt like a massive failure. But with a decade's perspective, and the knowledge that at least some of the company lives on as part of the Japanese technology conglomerate NEC, I can appreciate the lessons I learned from that disappointing period.

Some might see only that our timing was wrong. Yet wouldn't it be more fitting to emphasize how fortunate we were to participate in, and influence, an industry during a pioneering phase of the Internet? The misfortune of our failed IPO pales in comparison to the good fortune of our experience.

It is not a bad thing for successful people to fail at least once—and even to embrace failure. Not only will they gain valuable lessons, they can hardly fail to appreciate and savor future accomplishments.

Our Five Questions to Help Overcome "Failure"

☐ Was this really my True North?
☐ Was my own standard reasonable?
☐ Did I try everything possible to succeed?
☐ Am I being macromyopic and overdramatizing the short-term impact of the mistake?
☐ What can I learn from my "failure" (including: how do I make damn sure not to repeat this mistake)?

Was this really my True North?

Things fail sometimes. Why? Because you may not have cared enough. The fact is, highly capable people are often driven to meet external success standards that have little in common with what they truly want to accomplish. If you are working without meaning in a role, task, or job, your missing drive will make it harder for you to succeed. If you are conducting a post mortem of a failure, ask yourself, Was I truly self-motivated to succeed, or was someone (or something) else driving me to succeed?

If you were following your authentic True North—a goal, purpose, or calling you know you were born to follow—evaluate how and why things went awry. Being honest and aligned with your Heart and vision is perhaps the ultimate True North question.

Was my own standard reasonable?

Failure has much to do with internal expectations. If things don't go your way when you're launching a new strategy, or pitching a long-shot idea to a skeptical investor, don't relegate yourself gloomily to a future in middle management. Your expectations no doubt differ from others'. We recommend giving yourself a postfailure pep talk similar to one you'd give a new employee: *Don't sweat it—you're going to nail the next one.* Your inner voice shouldn't berate you any more than you would berate a hardworking employee.

Stretch yourself always, but never forget to calibrate your expectations. Research conducted on Olympic medal winners has found that athletes who won a bronze medal were actually happier than those who won a silver medal. It's easy to figure out why. Ex post, silver medalists fine-tune their internal standards against the dashed possibility of winning a gold medal, whereas bronze medalists are focused on the victory of standing on the Olympic podium and of turning in one of the three greatest performances in their sport. Ask yourself: Have you appropriately calibrated your failure?

Did I try everything possible to succeed?

How much effort did you put into your "failed" endeavor? Did you exhaust every conceivable approach in your quest for success?

If in evaluating yourself you find you didn't consider other ways to accomplish your goal, ask yourself why. If you were pessimistic about the outcome from the start, you could have saved yourself the time. As we noted earlier, optimism is an essential ingredient of Luck, and a bad attitude can become a self-fulfilling prophecy.

Am I being macromyopic and overdramatizing the short-term impact of the mistake?

Scientist Roy Amara has a great law: people tend to overemphasize the short-term effects of anything while underestimating the long-term impact. Which is another way of saying that most of us view the world through the lens of a sprint, forgetting we are actually running a marathon. This is *macromyopia*—overinflating and exaggerating the aches and pains of our near-term mistakes while discounting what we can learn from them in the future, or for that matter, whether they matter much in the long run.[17] Have a reality check on the real impact of your mistake. It may be invaluable long-term experience, or it may just not matter as much as you think.

What can I learn from my "failure" (including: how do I make damn sure not to repeat this mistake)?

Whether your recent failure was internally driven, externally driven, or a combination, use it as a learning opportunity. If you could start over, what would you do differently? How would your approach differ? Would you change everything, or simply tweak a few details? Be willing to take responsibility and admit, too, that you might not have succeeded even if you had performed flawlessly. Again, the key here is to address whatever failure you've experienced, explore it, learn from it, and don't repeat it.

"Our errors are surely not such awfully solemn things," philosopher William James once wrote. "In a world where we are so certain to incur them in spite of all our caution, a certain lightness of heart seems healthier than this excessive nervousness on their behalf."[18]

We couldn't agree more.

> In business, it is best to
> have long-term memory
> on experiences, short-term
> memories on feelings.
> —Dick Harrington

Last Words on Luck

If you take away nothing else from this chapter, we hope that it's this: Luck matters, and you can influence it. We are powerless to control Dumb Luck (though we tip our hat to you if it has played a role in your career), are generally at the whim of our Constitutional Luck (though we should take advantage of it), but can influence and increase our Circumstantial Luck.

Over the years, we haven't met many entrepreneurs who have succeeded due only to good fortune. That said, almost all great entrepreneurs and business-builders have had some degree of Luck on their side. Knowingly or unknowingly, they have managed to create or increase their capacity for Luck, thanks to careful preparation; a strong work ethic; and an optimistic, intellectually curious attitude tempered with humility and vulnerability.

Sometimes, despite all the Luck in the world, you will fail. The good news is, you are making mistakes because you are stretching. The bad news is, no one likes to fail. It's good to feel the pain. You want your mistake to bug you. Unless it hurts, you won't learn from it. Dick likes to say that there are two times when you should feel that pain. First is when the mistake or failure actually happens at that point, you want to feel bad. The second time is when you have to self-evaluate and ask, "What could I have done differently?" Add the learnings from that to your arsenal. After all, a failure is just a moment in time. If you learn the right lesson from your mistake, you won't make it again. It's an ongoing educational process. All experiences are good, including failures, assuming you are bright enough and smart enough to learn from them.

> *Experience is what you
> get when you didn't get
> what you wanted.
> —Randy Pausch* [19]

We don't advise anyone to become Luck-dependent. Like the other ingredients in this book, the role you permit Luck to play in your life optimally comes down to moderation and equilibrium. Avoid the gambler's fallacy of banking on future Luck to make up for your most recent losses. Be self-aware enough to distinguish between which accomplishments can be attributed to Luck and which you can chalk up to your own talents, skills, and capabilities.

As venture capitalist Patrick Chung notes, "I believe if you have Heart, Guts, and Smarts, you'll place yourself in the Lucky category—and you'll find yourself in those serendipitous situations that stem from being courageous and passionate."

In closing, we reach back again to William James, who wrote, "Man can alter life by altering his thinking." [20] Consider how humility, curiosity, optimism, vulnerability, authenticity, generosity, and openness have been magnets of positive ideas, circumstances, or relationships.

In short, don't depend on Luck for your success. But never bet against it, either.

CHAPTER IN SUMMARY

Luck's Inevitable Role in Business-Building

- The Role of Luck: Every business is affected by some element of Luck; external factors beyond our control are always at play. But despite its unpredictable nature, Luck is an undeniably necessary component of business success.

- Defining a Lucky Attitude: A Lucky Attitude = humility + intellectual curiosity + optimism. The combination of a Lucky Attitude with the right Lucky Network creates the possibility to influence certain types of Luck.

- Defining a Lucky Network: A subset of one's network that brings unforeseen positivity.

- Dumb Luck: Dumb Luck is the type of Luck over which we have no control. Its role is visible and appreciated only in hindsight.

- Constitutional Luck: The environment into which we're born can influence future interactions, predisposing us to certain opportunities and outcomes. These factors comprise Constitutional Luck, which brings leaders favorable and unexpected opportunities.

- Circumstantial Luck: Circumstantial Luck is about the situations in which we find ourselves. We can create and influence this type of Luck. It shows us how small or trivial events can lead to disproportionate and positive consequences.

- The Wisdom of Ignorance: Ignorance makes us oblivious to limitations, which can allow us to freely generate ideas that may ultimately make us more successful. It gives us an open mind and increases our convictions, stimulating our creativity and innovation.

- Humility: At the foundation of a Lucky Attitude is humility. Successful business-builders must be aware of their shortcomings. Humility and vulnerability humanize leaders, enhancing their ability to embrace Luck.

- Intellectual Curiosity: The capacity and desire to learn and see new things matter. People who explore, with the appetite to learn more about anything and everything, create and receive more Luck.

- The Energy of Optimism: An optimistic disposition gives entrepreneurs the belief that more, better, faster is always possible. Optimists energize any situation, always believing in the potential for better. A positive disposition increases the likelihood of seemingly "surprise" encounters of good fortune. Focus on the good before the bad.

- Fortune Within Lucky Networks: Lucky outcomes arise when uncertainty collides with something else. We can create an environment ripe with potentially favorable collisions by creating a thoughtful and expansive professional network.

- Bad Luck and Failure: Bad luck happens to everyone, and we can't let it bring us down. We have to learn from it and move past it.

6

BUSINESS
Archetypes AND Iconoclasts

Give musicians four notes, and they are capable of wildly different expressions. A musician gifted at syncopation may turn those notes into jazz, while another may create a beautiful symphonic phrase as part of a larger orchestration. The underlying four notes are the same, but each musician's implementation—via tweaks in sequencing, tonal quality, emphasis, and personal style—creates radically different expressions and results.

Similarly, the style in which entrepreneurial and business-building strengths combine can yield dramatically different results. Each of our four traits of Heart, Smarts, Guts, and Luck has a natural starting point that its owner can turn up or down, like a volume dial or an old-school stereo equalizer. We believe most people have the requisite baseline of Heart, Smarts, Guts, and Luck to build a business, as well as a capacity for realizing greater untapped potential in specific traits. Your HSGL profile isn't fated. It's in a state of continuous evolution based on increasing self-awareness and experiences gained. Taking the E.A.T. survey right now will yield an of-the-moment snapshot of your business-building preferences and decision-making biases, nothing more or less.

For entrepreneurs, then, the issue is less about the ins and outs of their HSGL constitutions than it is about gaining self-awareness and control of their HSGL potential during key points of the business-building cycle. This awareness and self-control is especially critical during what we have dubbed the *thresholds* of the growth cycle—those natural inflection points where a shift in gear is necessary (see figure 6-1, our classic growth-cycle pictogram).

In a March 2008 *Harvard Business Review* article, Matthew S. Olson, Derek van Bever, and Seth Verry of the Corporate Executive Board described the results of a study of what they labeled *stall points* across more than five hundred large companies. It turns out that at a certain point, typically after a long period of high-performance revenue growth, many companies hit a wall. Their growth falls precipitously, for reasons strategic and organizational.[1] This is intuitive and predictable, because it is much more a people question than one of market or other exogenous factors. The team that takes a business from A to B is not necessarily the best team to continue from B to C. We now want to explore how you can modulate your HSGL profile to best fit the right stage. Just as you showcase different parts of your personality depending on the audience, so too should your business-building strengths be matched to the operating context.

Successful entrepreneurs and business-builders have the capacity to shift gears. To continue this automobile analogy, while all racecar drivers know equally well how to operate a clutch and gearshift, it is the superstars who shift calmly, seamlessly, and powerfully through curves and obstacles. Arguably the most difficult skill for any business-builder to acquire is the capacity to adjust as needed, *when* it's needed, whether by evolving a leadership style and/or skills, or bringing on others to complement the gaps in their HSGL profile.

Consider, for example, the Heart-dominant founder. At the onset of a business, she is almost always the spark, the big bang, the inspiration. At the first growth threshold, between proof-of-concept and scaling up (that point between the first two S-curves of the growth cycle shown in figure 6-1), the Heart-dominant style of leadership requires a balanced dose of a Smart-Guts management. Similarly, those with high Smarts must be able at other points to shift to a Heart-, Guts-, or Luck-dominant gear in order to transform theories and inspirations into realistic execution. Truly great business-builders are able to orchestrate a fine balance across the HSGL spectrum, modulating these four traits whenever necessary.

Our goal in this chapter is to provide a broader overview of how at thresholds in the business-building cycles, Heart, Smarts, Guts, and Luck

FIGURE 6-1

Growth Cycle

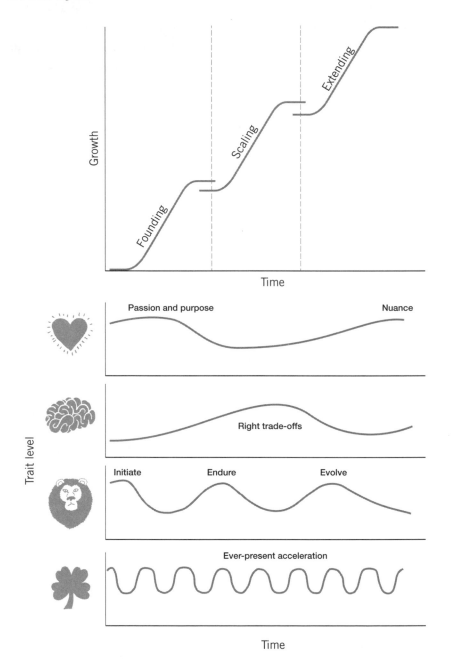

interact to form three common, unmistakable archetypes: the *founder*, the *scaler*, and the *extender*. The founder, scaler, and extender are not necessarily three different people. Founders and extenders often share similar profiles, while a small but impressive minority of entrepreneurs have played the role of both founder and scaler. Typically, though, we see these archetypal roles spread out across a team. For example, a scaler will often work closely with a founder, such as the Charlie Munger-Warren Buffett partnership in Berkshire Hathaway, or Fred Turner and Ray Kroc at McDonald's.

In this chapter, we will also focus on a unique character type that often cuts across all three types of business builders: the *iconoclast*. We define him as someone who not only plays across the spectrum of founding, scaling, and extending, but brings innovation to his business, a wildly untraditional perspective to the world, and disproportionate influence to his industry and even culture at large. Not surprisingly, iconoclasts are rare. We include them in this chapter to inspire readers and pay homage to those who dare to be great—whose success ripples well beyond their original intent.

The Business Archetype Growth Cycle

We can visualize how these archetypes relate to one another and help a business achieve its full potential and scale. Peter Drucker's classic S-curve is reimagined here—there is a jump between each phase and, accordingly, each business archetype. It's not always a smooth transition, but after an adjustment there is normally an inflection point of growth as the business—and its leader—get to the next level. In figure 6-1, a hypothetical HSGL timeline tracks the peaking HSGL traits in each archetype. While this varies from person to person, we hope this chart helps you take a look at where you stand across the archetypes and consider how your own HSGL peaks and valleys would look if plotted the same way.

Three Business Archetypes

As mentioned, there are three classic business archetypes—founder, scaler, and extender. We explore each one a little deeper in this section.

The Founder

Nearly 80 percent of the entrepreneurs and business builders who took our E.A.T. survey went by the title *founder* or *cofounder*. The most common HSGL profiles of these founders? Heart-Guts and Heart-Luck. Founders are the creators, innovators, and artists of the business world. As our Heart chapter attests, infectious enthusiasm and authentic passion are among the distinguishing hallmarks of Heart-dominant founders.

Earlier, we defined Guts-driven individuals as those who are not only able to push Heart-driven visions into reality, but are persistent and resilient enough to stay the course when things don't go perfectly to plan—which, we might add, is almost always. In the Heart-Luck paradigm, the secondary Luck trait exhibits both an optimism and an intellectual curiosity that is often a core ingredient of success. As an aside, it's worth noting that Luck-oriented folks were more likely to label themselves cofounders than founders—evidence of another hallmark of Luck; namely, humility.

Founders play a critical role at the beginning of the growth curve, where vision formation, team building, and cultural evangelism matter most. The best founders we know live and breathe one of our favorite Wisdom Manifestos Principles: *Think big, start small, and scale fast.*[2] By working closely and laterally across with all areas, from product development to HR to sales, they transmit their energy, vision, and conviction to the entire team.

That said, founders can find themselves bottlenecking a business at that first threshold between proof-of-concept and scaling up. Successful founders often face the rich-versus-king dilemma discussed in chapter 4, where a founder must ask himself what matters more: being in control of a small, successful organization or owning and operating (and sometimes adopting a different role within) a potentially larger, more impactful business.

Why do so many founders struggle to scale? There are several reasons, including blind loyalty to their cofounders, an inability to delegate responsibility and accountability, and a refusal to codify processes and operating metrics.[3]

As we have noted repeatedly throughout this book, the person who starts a business may not be the same person who gets you there in the end. Optimally, Heart-dominance pairs up with other characteristics, including Smarts, to advance a business to its next level. Enter the scaler phase.

The Scaler

The next phase of the growth cycle requires the traits of a scaler as much as, or in conjunction with, the characteristics of a founder. A scaler may be the same person as a founder, but most scalers work alongside, or even supplant, the founder. A scaler, who generally exhibits a Smarts-Guts profile, seeks impact by taking the *core* of a business idea to its next level, with the goal of creating more universal influence. Here, the word *core* is key. The scaler's objective is not to scale every single aspect of the founder's vision, but rather its *essence*. Typically, her goal is to make a mark on a broader swath of society, reaching and affecting far more consumers than the business currently attracts.

Along the way, she asks: *What trade-offs can we make?* She also seeks an enhanced understanding of consumers via qualitative and quantitative research and imposes tighter systems and operations. The scaler figures out end-user needs and opportunities that the founder may have bypassed, or never considered, and welcomes intelligent trade-offs between the core purpose of a founder's vision, and those noncore trade-offs will help the business swiftly advance to its next stage. Typically she boils the business down to three to five things on which she will never compromise; everything else she will shrewdly bargain in exchange for scale.

While founders often focus on how they can be the best at every aspect, scalers emphasize (or at least should emphasize) getting big in the right way. Needless to say, both goals are noble. The first sets the highest standards and integrity around a core vision. The second focuses on making the right trade-offs to create the maximal value-creating impact while minimizing negative cultural and vision aspects. In some rare instances, companies are able to be among the biggest *and* the best. Apple, to take an obvious example, is one of those rare companies that continues to achieve high impact and large levels of market value creation, while maintaining most of its exacting standards and intense focus on consumer-centricity and design. But this success has nonetheless required constant trade-offs.

The first image of the scaler that comes to mind is the "hired-gun" CEO or COO who plays in the steep slope of our classic S-curve growth pictogram. The defining characteristics of these leaders are the ability to set clear priorities, and to delegate and create performance-driven cultures through accountability at all levels of a firm. More nuanced are scalers' symbiotic relationships with the *spirit* of the founder, or of the founding phase, regardless of whether the founder is still in residence. The most successful scalers respect the past while focusing on the future. They are adept at both the left-brain exercises of priority-setting, delegation, and accountability *and* the right-brain activities of embracing a founder's inspiration and founding core principles while intuiting future customer needs and connecting with the emotion and personality of the brand, product, or service. Much of the scaler's job is to weigh the trade-offs between what needs to be kept from the past versus what needs to change for the future.

Scalers help companies endure. The very best scalers respect the founding principles and celebrate the institutional memory of the business, while inserting themselves to set and change direction and priorities for the sake of a firm's long-term vision. Successful scaler leaders exhibit a balanced distribution across our four HSGL traits—in the 20s (percent) for each characteristic. In short, the discipline and pragmatism of scalers complement the Heart of a business, and the optimal scalers at this growth stage are what we call *pragmatic idealists*.

Scalers do not lack Heart. They simply tend to be more muted, on a relative scale, with their Heart and louder with their Smarts and Guts.

Several notable examples of successful founder to scaler transitions come to mind—Pierre Omidyar to Meg Whitman at eBay; Larry Page and Sergey Brin to Eric Schmidt at Google (and at the time of writing, back to Page as the company looks to the extension phase of growth). There is, however, a much larger graveyard of blow-ups. All too often, would-be scalers fail to build from an existing foundation, or else they neglect to understand how a company attained its current success. These go for biggest but forget what had made them best. By ignoring these issues, some scalers can dissipate a company's spirit, often causing an exodus of very good people.

Venture capitalists are perennially faced with the dilemma of when to replace a founder-CEO. It becomes even more challenging when the situation is an either/or—for example, when a new CEO comes in and the founder leaves, or the founder stays with no new external CEO in place. A glance at the *Wall Street Journal*'s 2010 top fifty VC–backed companies finds that roughly half are led by founder-CEOs, while outside externally hired CEOs spearhead the others.[4] This ratio nicely represents the difficult dilemma as to who is best suited to lead a company to its potential. From our perspective, this choice shouldn't be either/or.

Since founder incumbents are by nature skeptical of new outside talent and influence, we have emphasized that successful scalers should embrace and *earn* the respect of founders by what they say and do, instead of trying to *command* respect via their positional authority. This is the same principle espoused in chapter 5 as part of the quality that makes for a Lucky Network. To facilitate this, a founder-scaler partnership should be in place long before a partnership is required. Founders who begin the business-building journey with a strong scaler, or who seek the right money when they need to scale alongside a partner who truly complements the leadership team (whether that partner is a new CEO, COO, or president) are more likely to succeed.

Organizations that can maintain a role for founders as a key ambassador, strategist, visionary (and yes, this might even mean CEO) while having a strong scaler in place are in a relatively stronger position. Also optimal would be a founder who can successfully transition to scaler, or who has a strong, trusted, longtime partner who focuses her attention on scaling.

But this is easier said than done; relationships between founders and scalers tend to move slowly at first. But letting ingredients cook slower toward a better meal isn't an altogether bad thing. Emerging academic evidence shows that when entrepreneurial founders stay with a company throughout its growth cycle—either in the top post or working in partnership with a strong operator/executor—those businesses perform better than their peers. The *microwave solution*—zapping a company toward faster, bigger growth, without fully understanding if that growth is right for the business—can satiate in the short-term but usually becomes something less than desirable over time.

We unfortunately see it too often, and frequently following a new investment. The microwave growth solution will go something like this: quickly assess the business, quickly hire a search firm, quickly get a new executive leader, quickly fire old founders, quickly get more people and more money, and quickly hope to sell. Sometimes it works, but rarely does it lead to something inspiring and great. Too quickly installing someone new and kicking someone else out (especially a founder) runs the risk of scrapping the inspiration and innovation that made the company what it is.

We encourage, wherever possible, the founder/entrepreneur to evolve to scaler and lead his company throughout as much of the entire growth cycle as possible. But that is the exception to the rich-versus-king dilemma—there are not a lot of rich kings. Of course, a few rare individuals, like Microsoft's Bill Gates, Chipotle Mexican Grill founder Steve Ells, and Amazon's Jeff Bezos, prove that it's possible in some cases to be both rich and king. If you think that's you too, go for it. But what is more realistic and the next-best option if you are not Superman? A situation in which a founder-scaler relationship has evolved over time, and where the founder is involved in selecting his or her new partner (and yes, new boss!) is a very good second choice. Cultural and professional compatibility between a founder and scaler is possible. And in those cases, percolating at a more measured pace toward long-term goals and purpose is more likely to create lasting value creation.

The Extender

The extender may have founded the business. She may even have scaled it to a certain point. But in contrast to the scaler, her mandate is to develop, expand, broaden, and even transform a business to its next stage. There comes a threshold in every business when after years of success, growth . . . slows. Blame everything from technology shifts, to changes in competitor and customer behavior, to complacent leaders. We have only to recall what online advertising did to newspapers, or what Amazon did to Borders, or how Apple's iPhone and Google's Android ascended seemingly overnight to the pinnacle of the smart-device market, significantly crippling RIM/ BlackBerry.

Extenders are adept at expanding into the next wave of innovation or growth. This could mean going into new country markets, creating adjacent applications, or radically reframing the business definition or the markets in which the company plays. Extenders are skilled at testing a company's preexisting assumptions and past successes, and repeatedly asking, intuiting, and testing: *What is it that customers really want, and what does that mean for my business definition (what business am I really in)?*

Indeed, the extender often plays the role of a transformer, as Dick did in moving Thomson from newspapers to information services. By speaking to countless end-users and asking that essential question *What business am I really in?* Dick realized a few things: that being in the newspaper business was less about publishing than advertising and that Thomson's capabilities made it more suited to move away from that business and toward information services. Similarly, Apple realized it was not in the computer business (in fact, the company officially dropped the word *computer* from its name), but was instead a media, entertainment, and personal device company.

Extenders can inject new life and growth into a company when it is most needed—from that middle high S-curve growth phase of success, to a wholly new S-curve. In this respect, extenders can be innovators in the sense famously defined by Clayton Christensen. They have an ability to figure out how their companies' greatest strengths mesh with the shifting competitive and market landscape. A common skill and characteristic of founders and extenders is the capacity to peer into the future and consider what it really means to be the best at something. This is also why founders sometimes leave and then return as extenders, as Steve Jobs and Howard Schultz did, respectively, at Apple and Starbucks.

The fact is, quite a few companies need to be episodically refounded. Recently, Google cofounder Larry Page returned to the post of CEO, shepherding the company as it explores its next horizon of growth. The HSGL makeup of extenders is therefore similar to that of founders: Heart-dominance, perhaps alongside a refined secondary Smarts trait (the increased ability to recognize patterns), or an experienced, time-tested, persevering secondary Guts trait.

Heart combined with the refined Smarts of experienced pattern recognition is a potent combination. *Why didn't we consider this before and what is next?* might well be the extenders' mantra. Their skill lies in their ability to envisage the business multidimensionally, to communicate clearly, and to pay close attention to what they see, in particular those discontinuities that create both threats and opportunities. Whether it is a new technology, a regulatory change, or altered trends in customer behavior, extenders embrace these shifts as a chance to jump to the next growth curve by defining the business and its market in wholly different ways. In figure 6-1, each S-curve represents a new wave of growth and opportunities. Extenders typically excel at leaping from curve to curve. Similar to founders, extenders can perceive or foresee opportunities that most might have deemed unlikely or even impossible.

This trait, the ability to perceive things differently and attempt the seemingly impossible, is native to the character type we profile next: the iconoclast.

The Iconoclast

As a game-changer, rule-breaker, and inspirational leader of the business world, the iconoclast is less a business archetype than a one-of-a-kind individual whose talents cut across the various stages of founding, scaling, and extending businesses. Iconoclasts view the world differently. They're unafraid to question norms or tackle problems in unfamiliar ways. Their singular approach and perspective allow them to approach a business with out-of-left-field insights and novel ideas. While we focus on the business iconoclast in this section, the iconoclast category encompasses many other fields—from the arts and sports, to government and academia. Think Chuck Close or Andy Warhol; Reggie Jackson or Mike Krzyzewski; Nelson Mandela or Lee Kuan Yew; John Kenneth Galbraith or Stephen Hawking.

In business, iconoclasts can be founders, scalers, or extenders. Regardless of their stage of involvement, they bring to the table a consistent, holistic philosophy of business to which they adhere throughout their careers. They can easily intuit what makes no sense or what strikes a false note. They also strive to reach an absolute standard of being the best in whatever they do. For iconoclasts, there is no such thing as an 80–20 rule. That is, finding the approximately correct answer is not the mind-set for their craft. They seek instead to be the most perfect perfectionist.

What is the singular, distinguishing trait of all great iconoclasts? Remember the three parts of the Heart definition? Purpose and passion, sacrifice, and finally, nuance. Let's revisit that third concept: *nuance*. In our experience, most great iconoclasts seek to become the best at something—and "the best" has its roots in authenticity, integrity, and alignment of purpose. But the greatness of iconoclasts comes not from executing on the 99 percent of things that others can functionally learn or perfect over time, but from the remaining 1 percent. Nuance, as we have noted, is subtle and barely discernible. No one can *see* it. But iconoclasts can *feel* it. Whether it's conscious or unconscious, nuance might thus be described as a highly evolved sixth sense.

In business, nuance is that "something" or "pixie dust" that creates unique differentiation. Nuance transports consumers by making the tangible the ordinarily intangible, the extraordinary. For Apple and its customers, it is the seamlessly wallpapered Apple experience: the art-gallery-like stores, the products, the white cool, the curvature, the precision, the quasi-religious iconography, the proprietary i-language, the treasurelike packaging. These elements are the result of maniacal attention to detail, but they are also the by-product of nuance, which transforms what might have been a tritely transactional experience into something multilayered, exultant, and yes, even beautiful.

In *Iconoclast: A Neuroscientist Reveals How to Think Differently*, Gregory Berns explains that the brain of an iconoclast is literally different from that of your everyday person. Most human brains are structured to interpret information as quickly and efficiently as possible, taking shortcuts as needed. Iconoclasts' brains, on the other hand, avoid such efficiency traps, finding ways to work around the brain's natural inclinations when synthesizing information. This alternative processing system allows them to see the world atypically and unconventionally.

While most people stick to the norm, iconoclasts seek novelty. Their contrarian or larger-than-life behavior may elicit its share of ridicule, but iconoclasts seldom let their own uncertainty or fear impede their behavior. Earlier we remarked that we know we are in the presence of Heart-dominant founders because of their infectious passion and purpose. Similarly, we know when we are in the presence of an iconoclast. A stubbornly different way of thinking has a funny habit of just plain jumping across the table at you. Remember the quote from chapter 4, "Stubbornness is great when you are right, but hell when you are wrong"? Iconoclasts may think differently, but the thing is, they're almost always *right*.

Deep in their natural dispositions, iconoclasts, like founders, tend to be exemplars of Heart with purpose and passion, yet they also have a pronounced ability to turn up and balance that Heart with extraordinary pattern recognition in their Smarts, resilience in their Guts, and intellectual curiosity and optimism (okay, maybe less humility) in their Luck.

Richard Branson, one of our favorite examples of an iconoclast, has a seemingly insatiable appetite for taking the unconventional path and pushing limits. The son of a lawyer and a flight attendant, Branson struggled in school as he battled dyslexia, but would go on to disrupt one industry after another. It is clear that his passion is not just for business but for living life to its highest potential. In 1986, his boat, the *Virgin Atlantic Challenger II*, crossed the Atlantic Ocean in the fastest time ever recorded. A year later Branson made the first hot-air-balloon crossing of the same ocean. Limits-testing adventures are only one half of his iconoclasm. Branson has also bucked convention in his business endeavors, usually out of deep personal passion. From record-label mogul, to airline CEO, to the visionary behind a much bigger lifestyle brand, to space travel pioneer, his endeavors have reflected a deep desire to reshape industries and a willingness to bet repeatedly on something novel and bigger. He relentless dares to be great at the expense of his track record. Yet he has built a spectacular track record.

Much has been written about Steve Jobs, and much more will be. Here we mention him not only because he is such a great case study, but because his absence in a section on iconoclasts would be conspicuous. The orphan turned tech boy wonder will be remembered for a long time for his ability to think big and yes, think different. His track record in leading and shaping industries through Apple, NeXT, and Pixar cements his reputation as one of the greatest-ever iconoclastic business leaders. Jobs's iconoclasm may best be defined by an attitude that he described in his 2005 commencement address at Stanford: "If today were the last day of my life, would I want to do what I am about to do today?" While such a quote coming from almost anyone else might be viewed as the trite, saccharine stuff so common in commencement talks, from Jobs there was an authenticity—a genuine attitude and way of living behind this statement that made it resonate. And in a similar fashion, two of the other quotes from this iconoclast that went almost instantaneously viral after his death:

> "Insanely great." Jobs used this phrase to describe the Macintosh computer and often thereafter in challenging people to become insanely great in everything they do.

> "Do you want to sell sugar water for the rest of your life or do you want to come with me and change the world?" This is what Jobs asked John Sculley in recruiting him to Apple.

Jobs, iconoclastic? Yes.

While iconoclasts are most likely to be founders, they can also be corporate leaders and change agents. On the founder side, think of Henry Ford, Jeff Bezos (Amazon), Walt Disney, and Akio Morita (Sony). On the transformative business-builder side, think of Jack Welch (GE), Katharine Graham (*Washington Post*), Lou Gerstner (IBM), and Ray Kroc (McDonald's), to name just a few. Or consider couturier Coco Chanel, who prided herself on creating fashion at a different level than the rest. Chanel's meticulous attention to detail was evident in her insistence on placing quilting in women's jackets, and even sewing weights into her hemlines, so that wearers, who were often in the public eye, never had to fear a Marilyn Monroe–style gust of wind.

In the iconoclast category, we also place winemaker Helen Turley, who has always been several steps ahead of the rest of the grape industry. In 1991, Turley's decision to plant grapes on the then-undiscovered Sonoma Coast led to the founding of Marcassin Vineyard, which today produces some of California's most renowned Pinot Noirs and Chardonnays. A purist and a perfectionist, Turley had the courage to challenge and ultimately redefine how vintners manufactured and created wine.

We call out Turley because it is important to emphasize that iconoclasts don't always have to create the world's largest enterprises. They do, however, almost always seem to hold themselves to the highest bar in their respective fields. Through her creations and leadership, Turley, like all the other iconoclasts we have discussed, is almost certain to leave behind an enduring fingerprint. Why? She simply loves what she does and wants to be the best at it.

It's what we should all strive for.

CHAPTER IN SUMMARY

Business Archetypes and Iconoclasts

- Taxonomy of Business Creation and Business-Building Profiles: We have seen three key business archetypes: the founder, the scaler, and the extender. (They are not necessarily three different people.) These archetypes correlate to the typical S-curve growth cycles of a company.

- Founders: Typically Heart-dominant, most commonly with a secondary trait of either Guts or Luck. Founders play a critical role at the beginning of the growth curve, where vision formation, team building, and cultural evangelism matter most.

- Key reasons founders fail to scale: Desire for control over progress (and inability to delegate responsibility); misplaced collegial loyalty; absence of systems and processes.[5]

- Rich-versus-king: The trade-off between building value in a smaller role or playing a larger role in a smaller company that most founders must face as they scale. (The term was popularized by HBS professor Noam Wasserman.)

- Founder to scaler transition: Founders should either recognize the need for a scaler counterpart long before one is needed (and begin working together in advance) or, when the time comes, have enough self-awareness and confidence to evolve to a more delegatory role.

• The Scaler: Often embodying a Smarts-Guts profile, the scaler is typically a growth-oriented business-builder. She has to understand what core elements of a founder's culture to preserve and what elements she can trade off for the purposes of scale.

• The Extender: A strong Heart with refined Smarts pattern recognition.

- Asks repeatedly: *What business is the company really in?*

- Reframes the marketplace and business definition to explore new frontiers for the business

- Extenders and founders can be one and the same, as they share similar qualities to start and restart a business

• Iconoclasts: An extreme (and rare) breed of game-changers and rule-breakers with an uncanny sense of purpose and strength across the HSGL spectrum. With a reach that goes beyond their own business and industry, they profoundly affect present-day and future cultures and leave behind a historical fingerprint via their creations and leadership.

7

PUTTING *It* All TOGETHER

We have stressed the importance of self-awareness throughout this book, believing strongly it is crucial to your professional (and life) success. By knowing where your predispositions lie, and when to dial down or amplify those traits, you will go a long way toward enhancing your business-building future. Through self-awareness and reflection, you better understand why you made such decisions.

We hope our descriptions of the four core HSGL traits have directed you to a greater understanding of your natural biases and tendencies. The results of the Entrepreneurial Aptitude Test, or E.A.T.—online at www.hsgl.com or in abbreviated form in chapter 10 of this book—will give you a directional idea about what natural bias with which you lead.

Every entrepreneur and business-builder of our acquaintance possesses a relative mix of Heart, Smarts, Guts, and Luck. But how does this mix correlate to the natural cadence common to virtually all businesses? Because enterprises pass through shared, natural, and continual thresholds or inflection points—which most leaders commonly tend to recognize only in retrospect—this chapter explores the business-building DNA that companies require at each stage of growth and what to do if you find yourself coming up short.

First, let's briefly revisit our four core HSGL traits.

Heart

As a Heart-dominant person, you are driven by purpose, passion, sacrifice, and all the nuances toward making something exceptional. You are prepared to expend time, effort, and hard work to attain your goals. Your vision is contagious and simply won't quit. Moreover, your desire to transform society means almost more to you than your concept or product, and you value the intrinsic compensations of what you do as much as you do the extrinsic rewards.

A Heart-dominant visionary moves forward with confidence and urgency. She lacks the luxury of having all the facts at hand. She knows no perfect time exists to roll out a business. But she is hungry—almost obsessive—to share her vision, purpose, and passion with the rest of the world.

Smarts

Smarts may come in the form of Book Smarts, Street Smarts, People Smarts, or Creative Smarts. Ideally, you bring these elements together to create what we call Business Smarts, giving you an intuitive understanding of when to dial up or dial down each kind of Smarts.

What makes your Business Smarts stand out? Your ability to recognize patterns easily and early on, whether they're based on metrics, trial and error, long-term experience, or knowledge of human behavior. You are just better than the rest at pattern recognition. By zooming in and out, often in a split second, you're able to frame analogies and storylines that others may be slower to grasp. Your skill in recognizing patterns in turn creates practical, repeatable habits that in time become automatic and apply directly to successful future business-building.

Guts

When the path ahead requires bold and sustained action, you're the candidate for the job. You have no problem making a tough call, sticking to an unpopular decision, following a grueling work ethic, and managing risks. You have the Guts to Initiate, the Guts to Endure, and the Guts to Evolve.

We hear it all the time: "I have a great idea, it's just that . . ." or "I know I'm an entrepreneur, I just haven't come up with that killer idea." There follows a cascade of good reasons why not. Without the necessary Heart and Guts to take an idea and run with it—while surrounding yourself with the best people—you are just not an entrepreneur. Hatching a winning concept means little if it is not executed and transformed into reality. Otherwise your idea will remain an intellectual romance.

Luck

Things often work out for you—whether via fortuitous relationships, unexpected opportunities, or sheer happenstance. You have probably influenced your own good fortune by remaining grounded, having an inquisitive mind, and being more optimistic and positive than the rest. This is your Lucky Attitude, rooted in humility, intellectual curiosity, and optimism. This attitude combines with closely related traits of vulnerability, authenticity, generosity, and openness to create and maintain a Lucky Network that ultimately enhances your success. Attitude and relationships really do make a big difference.

But while a Lucky Attitude mapped to a well-tended Lucky Network can ignite opportunities, if you lack the Heart to engage or the Smarts to make your way forward, your ability to interact with good fortune may be worth very little. When Luck comes your way, you need to be able to act on it with your Heart, Smarts, and Guts.

Heart, Smarts, Guts, and Luck

Our HSGL framework is a work in continuous refinement. Frameworks are by nature impositions on chaos, and we're often skeptical of them ourselves. We recognize that the ingredients that comprise business-builders and business developers are pretty complex. That said, we hope that the chapters up to this point have introduced you to a simplified vocabulary of entrepreneurship that helps you identify your individual strengths and potential weaknesses and the natural biases you have in decision making. It may even help you understand how best to work with other people as you become aware of their HSGL profile and how to make better future decisions by better comprehending why you made past ones.

The E.A.T. survey is our attempt at helping you figure out where exactly you stand—and helping us classify the entrepreneurs and business-builders we have encountered through the years. It's not exhaustive, but the results are directionally correct. There are no right or wrong answers on the E.A.T. survey, nor is there a numeric standard business-builders have to meet. The test is designed to suss out which way you lean, not whether you have the baseline amount of Heart, Smarts, Guts, or Luck needed to start or build a business. We use it as one core input for helping people develop better self-awareness, and it naturally needs to be used in conjunction with other approaches. We want to make sure that readers do not confuse the four HSGL core traits for a how-to business-building checklist. Life and entrepreneurship are not that clean or simple. So relax. Don't beat yourself up if you find yourself lacking in any one trait. Use the HSGL results as guideposts and mirrors to what you know are your strengths and weaknesses.

Over the years we have come across exceptional people in the business world—Mozarts of enterprise and commerce, as it were. Though obviously varying in their HSGL makeup, these individuals are so talented at what they do that whatever mixture of traits they bring to their business-building endeavors carries the day. Any shortcoming they might have in a single area is overwhelmed by the sheer potency of their mix or a spike in one or two of the traits.

Most of us lack that sheer genius. Vanishingly few people have the capacity to create and sustain a business on the scale of, say, an Amazon or an Apple. Yet many smaller and lesser-known businesses are still immensely successful. We just need to step back from time to time and reconsider what it means to be successful; it is a highly personal question. Success should not and cannot be measured just by financial metrics and sheer size; impact, quality, and fulfillment of purpose are as important. With what Tsun-yan refers to as the three Ds—discipline, dedication, and diligence—most of us can make steady upward professional progress toward our personal goals. Whether that is becoming the best specialized Web-app shop, an independent movie studio, or a single destination restaurant—versus, respectively, a global development services firm, the biggest next-generation mega-movie studio, or a chain of thousands of a new quick service restaurants—all can be noble pursuits worth doing.

Your business venture will also have its own set of core trait requirements. Certain HSGL profiles are better suited to certain concepts than others. For example, the food and restaurant industries might draw in Heart-Luck-dominant people, whereas an individual who leads with Smarts is far more likely to hatch the concept of, say, manufacturing a new line of hybrid automobiles. Our research is still evolving in this area, but over time, we believe we will see more correlations between HSGL profiles and industries as our survey-taking population grows.

Even more important than the differences across industries are the striking consistencies. Businesses in every sector go through similar stages of growth and confront similar challenges. What is most crucial is understanding why, when, and how those with particular HSGL leanings flourish or flounder at critical growth junctures.

Where Heart Flourishes

Heart-dominance is most common and critical during the ideation or founding of a company. During these conceptualization phases, a strong Heart forms the basis of a belief system around the company's purpose and vision. The Heart inspires and attracts people to help build the vision into a reality. The Heart-dominant entrepreneur's obsession with trying to perfect her vision is almost druglike to herself and those around her. Within this context, the Heart-driven individual feels out what her market is and who her customers are, but it is her ongoing infectious passion that draws people to her.

Most commonly we see the Heart-Guts combination in the founder or progenitor of a product or venture, in part because of the passion and perseverance needed to bring an idea into the world. But the challenges for Heart-dominant individuals show up even at a venture's inception. During the start-up, for example, a visionary, Heart-driven founder may not have the time or patience needed to tend to paperwork, controls, or systems.

The limitations of the Heart become even more apparent when it comes time to scale a company—whether it's acquiring more clients, expanding the breadth of operations, building an organizational infrastructure, or establishing additional controls and systems. Heart-driven founders may lack the capacity to delegate or implement processes. Market realities often conspire to create a challenging context for a Heart-driven purpose or passion. At the end of the day, a founder or visionary has to face the commercial reality of whether customers want or don't want her product. Key to the long-term success of the Heart-driven founder is building an appropriate team, entrusting its members with responsibility, and then balancing idealism with excellence in scaled execution.

This is where the Smarts-dominant person comes in.

Where Smarts Flourishes

During the scale-up phase, the Heart-driven founder frequently bumps up against her own limitations. In some cases, she may be too much of a visionary to focus her efforts on day-to-day operations. As the business achieves a proof of concept, acquires additional clients, expands operations, builds an organizational infrastructure, and establishes widespread controls and systems, bringing in a Smarts-dominant person can be essential.

Ultimately, the capacity to cope with change is one of the Smarts-driven person's greatest strengths. For this reason, while she has the potential to be a good founder, she's often most formidable as a pivoter or scaler of businesses.

Having said that, we must add, Smarts-dominant people can be consumed with attaining perfect knowledge before acting. As more information surfaces later, they tend to second-guess themselves. Analytically oriented minds occasionally find solace in academic approaches and theories, when what really matters is a grounded practicality in the market. Finally, certain intellectually driven individuals may also unwittingly intimidate others, dismissing some of the softer aspects of business- or culture building. Therefore, like other trait-driven individuals, Smarts-dominant people should be self-aware enough to complement their skills, continuously test their own practicality, and be prepared to act swiftly as the situation warrants.

This sets the stage for Guts.

Where Guts Flourishes

As a Guts-dominant individual, your "get things done" attitude complements your stoicism. Your attitude derives from your ability to manage and mitigate risks, maintain an even keel in occasionally challenging conditions, and evolve the business as the market environment demands. With the soul of the business strong, you can focus on extending that same soul into the world. For this reason, you have the potential to be either a good pivoter or scaler.

At times, however, Guts-dominant people may take on too much risk with insufficient information or drive forward without fully considering the softer aspects of the decision. What's more, Guts-dominant individuals have to beware the propensity to always move forward with action without fully embracing Heart-driven values, the bigger picture, or the nuances of a founder's overall vision. Among the characteristics of a successful Guts-oriented leader is the capacity to step back, especially for longer-term strategic considerations, and the ability to remain open to the complementary modes of thinking of Heart- and Smarts-driven individuals.

Enter the art of being Lucky.

Where Luck Flourishes

Luck acts to accentuate the impact of our other three traits. Good fortune derives from a lifelong attitude of humility, intellectual curiosity, and optimism. This Lucky Attitude is intricately linked to and in many ways responsible for a Lucky Network, or a broader relationship base of fortuitous connections that help advance one's career or personal goals. All business-builders have some degree of luck on their side, thanks to a Luck-oriented attitude and the ability to form and take advantage of strategic relationships that a Luck-oriented disposition affords them.

But no entrepreneur should rely solely on Luck to start, scale, or extend his business. For all that we can do to foster Circumstantial Luck, we must remember that, by its very nature, Luck can at best be influenced and cannot be governed. Similarly, for every moment of good Luck there is a period of bad Luck. Whether in the form of a simple mistake, missed opportunity, or total failure, bad Luck plagues everyone. But it is important for anyone in the position of failure to remember that how you deal with it, not the failure itself, is what distinguishes you. Overcoming, learning through, and bouncing back from a failure all help you develop as a leader.

Luck should be a thread that weaves throughout the tapestry of your professional life and the various business cycles. What is important is ensuring that at all stages you control the role Luck plays by maintaining a Lucky Attitude and Network—and, critically, that you are self-aware enough to know when to attribute accomplishments to Luck versus your own talents and skills.

Understanding the Limitations of Your HSGL Profile

Your HSGL profile is a snapshot of you today, and you can very well tweak or adapt it. The greatest entrepreneurs and leaders are those who can adapt their profiles or, if that is not possible, their environment, when the time is necessary. This flexibility ensures that the skills and traits necessary at specific moments and inflection points of a business rise to the top. But this flexibility does not always come naturally. Like a muscle, it needs to be trained. Below is a four-point plan on how to train and, at times, supplement your HSGL muscle to adapt and shift as your business grows and changes.

1. Really (We Mean Really) Understand Your Profile. Let's face it, we all like to focus on our strengths. So when you review your HSGL profile, it is likely you will spend most of your time on understanding and accepting your strengths. But that is only half of the picture. To truly assess who you are, you must also embrace and come to terms with the areas in which you are weak. Now is the time to ask yourself: *Where are the areas in which I am the most vulnerable? If I had a fatal flaw, what would it be? Was there anything that surprised me?* This self-awareness of both the good and "the bad and the ugly" is a starting point for optimizing your capabilities and working around your weaknesses. Take the E.A.T. survey, reflect on the True North questions, and think back on your own experiences. Success comes equally from knowing your strengths as it does from accepting, anticipating, and addressing your weaknesses.

2. Determine the Best Behavior for the Time and Context. The first part of this four-part plan is an emphasis on the *what* side of your profile and understanding what gaps you are likely have. The second part of the plan asks you to consider the time and context to identify the behaviors and underlying traits required to succeed.

Behaviorist B. F. Skinner conducted a famous experiment in which he provided caged pigeons with a mechanism that delivered them peanuts at intervals according to their level of pecking. Skinner's pigeons soon discovered that repeated pecking yielded more results and began to increase their pecking rate. Likewise, most people quickly become conscious of the behaviors that yield them the best results—and behave that way more often.[1]

At a certain point, though, Skinner's machine ran out of nuts. Pecking stopped yielding success, so the pigeons ceased their pecking, recognizing that their efforts would be in vain. Humans also gradually become aware they have reached their own natural frontiers or boundaries. The same goes for business-builders—there is a certain point at which a specific behavior just won't deliver the desired benefit. At these moments, do you have the ability to identify what new behaviors will add value? Ask yourself: What behavior will yield the very best results? Will something that worked in the past still work in future? Are my strengths aligned with the optimal behavior? This last question is critical, and often ignored. If the behavior needed in this specific context does not align with your HSGL profile strengths, success becomes more elusive. The next two points offer some guidance on how to address this.

3. Train for the Optimal Behavior: Focus on Your Backhand. Just as an athlete must practice to improve his game, business-builders can develop and systematically strengthen the traits required for certain behaviors. With an awareness of your profile and an assessment of the requirements of a specific business situation, you can incrementally improve and in some cases even step-function improve some of the areas where you may have failure points. The natural bias for people is to lean and train toward their strengths—if someone is killer in tennis doing down-the-line forehands, you often see him repeating training on that strength. Don't fall in to the trap of avoiding your "backhand." If you look to the first two principles in this section (knowing where your limitations are and in what situations they will hurt you), then practice to improve that weakness.

At a mundane level there are traits that can be markedly improved with training—for example, improving communication skills, a critical attribute for projecting confidence and inspiration. One of the first things to do is to identify all the big bucket elements that can easily be trained: communication and presentation; or calendar and time management.

But many cases, especially on the soft-skill side, call for more artful or nuanced development and more radical measures. You may need to go so far as to fundamentally reconstruct your approach to leading people. This may mean understanding how to gather perceptions people have of you and the situation and whether or not they are right, recognizing that their reality is their perception. Understanding the artful way to transition some of the solution from you to the group, or appreciating how to leverage a business coach or mentor appropriately for counsel is key for these situations. Here we differentiate between receiving *counsel* and receiving *advice*. A golf professional giving you advice generally focuses on one thing, then tells you what to do about it: *Keep the club more flat toward the top of the swing. Take more putting lessons.* A person giving you counsel will ask a different set of questions: *What do you envisage prior to and after you contact the ball? How can we improve the approach you bring to your game? Do you really enjoy competitive golf?* It comes down to the difference of getting a true master and counselor versus a technical trainer. Both can help, but a great mentor/counselor thinks about your bigger picture and best interests as much as specific, skill-based improvements. Ensure that you have a council of mentors and opportunities and, if you are early in your career trajectory, consider how best to take on apprenticeship positions that allow you to shadow those whom you respect most. Be willing to put yourself into situations where you know your limits will be tested; accept that situation and make yourself vulnerable to potential failure. Again, the more you can do this earlier in your business-building career, the better.

4. Complement and Supplement Your Profile. There are times, however, when you won't be able—because of time constraints, context, or personal capacity—to train toward new behaviors. In these moments, the best solution is to either complement or supplement your profile with external resources.

By *complementing* your profile, you are buttressing yourself and your business with other people whose HSGL profile is strong where yours is lacking. If, as we believe, our weaknesses are our strengths, and our strengths are our weaknesses, now is the time to fill in those places where you find a shortfall. This starts, again, with knowing yourself and being willing to surround yourself not just with excellence but the right diversity of excellence that can help get the job done better and faster.

By *supplementing* your profile, you take in another person who brings strengths similar to yours to the table. This is especially important when a business wants to scale. Other times, it may be important if you are without a business "soul mate." As we have shared and as other leaders have chronicled, positions at the top are lonely, isolating, and often misunderstood. The value of a peer who "gets it" like you do can be a critical support mechanism, advocate, and trusted copilot for greater leverage.

In either case, it is critical to allow these resources to rise and take action when you are not capable.

With a deeper understanding of each of the HSGL traits that help drive entrepreneurship, we now shift our attention to see what other strategies and tools can help you increase the odds of business-building success. Starting with the next chapter, we focus on providing questions for self-reflection and some practical wisdom and habits.

⑧

TRUE NORTH *Questions* *for Reflection*

Now we return to our emphasis that self-awareness is the critical starting point for success. This chapter consists of ten sets of True North questions designed to spur reflection and reveal important facets of both you as the business-builder and your business itself.

1. What Is Really Holding You Back? (Heart)

2. On Vision and Purpose (Heart)

3. On Assumptions, Beliefs, and Values (Heart)

4. Getting the Right Mix of Smarts (Smarts)

5. Do You Need a Strategic Checkup? (Smarts)

6. On Guts (Guts)

7. To Sell or Not to Sell? (Guts)

8. Are You Humble Enough? (Luck)

9. Creating Luck with Optimism and Relationships (Luck)

10. Reflecting on Failure

Pick and choose the sets of questions that resonate most with you. Each True North question set consists of a central topic followed by four or five related queries to help you reflect on that topic. By assembling them here for easy reference, we hope that you come back to them from time to time. We even encourage you to tear them out, dog-ear the pages, or mark them up. The questions in this chapter and the Wisdom Manifestos Principles in chapter 9 are meant to be an evergreen reference section—so go at it with your Post-it tabs, your red pens, highlighters, or X-Acto knives. (That is, as long as you actually own this copy of the book!)

In the end, we hope to inspire a penchant for reflection by providing a guided framework for doing so along some key dimensions covered in this book. If nothing more, these True North question sets make for good conversation starters with colleagues—and they may even allow you to skip bringing in an outside facilitator for your next team offsite!

#1: What Is Really Holding You Back?

What is really holding you back from starting your venture? Ask yourself these questions to see whether the issue is a need to gain clarity on the idea, revolves around people problems, or masks a more fundamental self-doubt.

1. Are you waiting for "the perfect time" to launch your business? Entrepreneurship isn't something you plot, devise, schedule, re-schedule, or delay. You cannot in vitro fertilize a great business. If it is in your Heart, the perfect time is now.

2. Are you a bond or an equity? Are you willing to swap certainty to pursue passion, meaning, and purpose? Or will your practical, realistic side impel you toward more conservative choices? Many would-be entrepreneurs are eager to start something, but struggle with trade-offs like debt, family, personal lifestyle, etc. Ultimately, it is difficult to have your cake and eat it, too: *The higher the risk, the higher the reward* is just how the equation works. Most

would-be entrepreneurs like to think of themselves as equities but act more like bonds.

3. Do you believe you're an entrepreneur, but you just don't have a great idea yet? Then you're not an entrepreneur. Furthermore, it is always better to focus on the right people than on the right idea. Get the right people with whom you want to work and go with an idea that you viscerally feel is connected to your purpose and passion.

4. Do you like your idea, but have no idea how it will make money? The "build audience first, monetize later" strategy popular today in technology and social media *can* work, but very few pull it off. The reality of how a company eventually makes money will become crucial sooner than most entrepreneurs realize. The best source of future fundraising, after all, is to earn it.

5. Which is your weakest link among passion, capabilities, and market acceptance? In chapter 2, we describe the magic that occurs when passion, capabilities, and market acceptance all intersect. What are you most passionate about, and where do you have the greatest comparative advantage? Reflect deeply on your Heart and capabilities, then see if those two things map to an attractive commercial market. Of these three elements, which is your strongest and weakest component?

#2: On Vision and Purpose

It is sometimes easy to drift away from the authentic vision that started it all. Ask yourself these anchoring questions to re-center your feelings and hone your purpose.

1. Did you begin with a business plan—or with Heart? People with strong Heart are compelled not just to build a business, but to share their purpose and vision with the world. Most great busi-

nesses start off as passion-driven initiatives. Surprisingly (or maybe not) few begin with a business plan. Many founders start with a series of "passion projects" that eventually find their way to the right market. In this sense, early iterative trial is often the basis for a more informed business plan.

2. Are you confusing ideas with Heart? Merely hatching a winning concept doesn't mean an individual is entrepreneurial, at least not in the way we define the term. Without relentless execution toward making an idea a reality, most ventures are short-lived. As an inborn belief system and a lifelong mission, genuine entrepreneurship requires taking a great idea and then taking the necessary execution steps to get aloft.

3. If money did not matter, would this be what you would be doing? Are you doing what you're doing out of love and the desire to make a difference—or are you in it for the money? The answer most often lies somewhere in between. The bigger point is, if you're seized by an intrinsic and almost artistic compulsion to bring to life a vision that won't quit, think hard about how you can do it.

4. Are you continually asking yourself "Why?" You should be. There is power in Heart and purpose. Both point to the necessity of launching a business by addressing the *why* before the *how*. As Mats Lederhausen says, "Purpose before product, and product before profit." He means that purpose, and the product that ultimately emerges from it, are what ultimately drive profit. That purpose is the *why*.

5. Does your idea, decision, or initiative "feel" right? By recommending that entrepreneurs answer this very simple question, we can measure much of the very meaning of Heart. In the first stages of business-building, you lack the luxury of having all the facts at hand. Nor do you (or anyone for that matter) possess the ability to see deep into the future. You just need to ask: *Do I know what is right? Can I trust what I am feeling?*

#3: On Assumptions, Beliefs, and Values

An individual's Heart must ultimately reflect a set of assumptions, beliefs, and values—in that order. Below is a recap of these concepts and some related questions to help understand how these factors relate in your own life.

Our *assumptions* are conscious and explicit understandings and perceptions about our world.

Our *beliefs* spring from these assumptions. They are our conjectures about what would happen in potential scenarios, based on what we understand via our assumptions. For example, one belief might be that if worse comes to worst, we have access to financial support from friends or family that could sustain us personally or professionally.

A *value* is a belief and assumption that circumstances have never challenged or disproved. These are deep-rooted principles that underpin Heart.

1. What assumptions are you bringing to your business-building journey? Do you need (or presume) the existence of certain support networks? Are you relying on the economy for a certain degree of stability or growth? What assumptions do you have that aren't going to change in the foreseeable future? For example, to what extent are things like your health, the economy, specific trends, the friendship between cofounders, or other personal factors truly guaranteed?

2. What belief set are you holding onto for your Plan A or B? If everything goes right or even beyond your expectations, what beliefs surround your business? Similarly, if things do not go according to Plan A, what beliefs underlie your Plan B? If you don't get the equity financing, are you counting on the availability of convertible debt? Are you assuming you have sufficient incentives to retain employees or that you can readily replace certain key people?

3. What are the most crucial values of your business? Values are the soil nutrients that permit the plant that is your business to grow and thrive. They represent the core principles that support your overall purpose. Can you articulate the values of your business?

4. Who is living your values today? The people on the front line of your business must embody the company's mission and values. If your company emphasizes happiness, but your employees are miserable, you have lost the linear connection between the Heart of the founder or the CEO and the individuals who breathe that value.

5. What are you prepared to do when those values are violated? Economic pressures or changes in the financial climate can often force a company to breach its own core values. There are trade-offs in any company when it elects to scale up. It is just impossible to keep every element of a highly controlled, small organization the same at large scale. Again, it is important to question if you want that scale and to understand if you are willing to trade off certain values of the product or service as a cost to scale. If not, are you comfortable with the potential size that the business can achieve in its current configuration? Do you care more about getting money to scale, or is waiting and delaying plans to get the right money more important? To what values must you remain uncompromisingly true?

#4: Getting the Right Mix of Smarts

Take a step back and reframe your conception of not just your own cognition but also some key aspects of your business. Here, these Smarts-oriented approaches to business challenges can lend new insight.

1. Are you naturally biased toward left-brain or right-brain thinking? We mentioned psychobiologist and Nobel Prize–winner Roger W. Sperry's right-brain/left-brain divide in chapter 3. The difference

between these two modes of thought is significant, so consider: are you more left-brain driven (comprehensive, analytical, rational) or right-brain driven (visual, conceptual, holistic)? More important than the actual answer is (1) that you are aware of whatever natural bias you have, and (2) that you are open to complementary perspectives from the other side.

2. What is the (right-brained) essence of your business model? The business world veers naturally toward left-brained thinking. Yet roughly 90 percent of our decisions and our preferences are emotional (only afterward do we justify them based on their practicality or functionality). So ask yourself: *What are the emotional components of your business that will excite or engage a potential investor or consumer?*

3. What are the most critical facts and metrics that support your idea and business model? Focus on the three or four most critical facts that would help you further validate your idea. Know very specifically how you will measure if you are "winning." Understanding how you will judge your progress on both the input side (leading indicator metrics) and the output side (desired performance/financial metrics) matters critically. We are partial to input metrics, which are the leading indicators to performance and usually pertain to customer happiness. If a customer is happy, the output metrics (i.e., financial results) tend to follow.

4. What is the most pragmatic way you can attack your business intent? What if you only had $100? How would you get started? The essence of entrepreneurship is making things happen with the little you have. Step back and consider the shortest distance between your current position and a key milestone for your idea or business. How might you get there cheaper, faster, better? Force yourself to avoid theories and *ifs*. Think instead about what you would do if you had only forty-eight hours to act. Chances are you may need less organizational baggage or planning than you think. One example that comes to mind was a start-up focused on bringing natural food into the workplace. The team was initially focused on all the suppliers they needed to get on board, and how

to convince them of this new vision for healthy snacks at work. The vision was right—they were thinking big—but they wanted to also start big. We encouraged them to start small instead with a series of simple market tests. They reprioritized and simply bought their supplies at Whole Foods for the first couple of months to see if people would indeed substitute mindful choices for unhealthy foods. Sequencing here was key. Before locking in and spending time on large supplier deals, find out if the customer really wants the product. Such a test can be done quickly and cheaply and provides disproportionate insights.

5. Have you considered the ten people who would be game-changers for your business? A common mistake we have seen over the years involves perceiving the potential roles at a company in terms of its current trajectory. To be sure, that's helpful in understanding what you need tomorrow, but how can you think about the talent that will really make your business sing? Make a list of ten exceptional individuals, and what would happen if they were involved with your business and able to take it to the next level. It doesn't matter if you know these ten people already or not.

Now, build a people pipeline and work at it relentlessly. Just as most "overnight successes" are a decade or more in the making, so too are talent-cultivation efforts. Create an all-star list and start getting to know those people *today*, building long-term relationships that will enable you to recruit them in the future when the opportunity arises.

#5: Do You Need a Strategic Checkup?

Sometimes companies need to step back and ask themselves if they understand what is really driving good or bad performance. You can use the contemporary jargon—*Let's see if we need to pivot*—or call it a *strategic review*. Our advice? Start with the customer. With the customer in mind, your answers to this set of questions can help you ascertain if you need to step back and reassess. If the answer to any of them is yes, it may be time to do a deep dive on getting to know your customer.

1. Is your market experiencing a discontinuity? *Discontinuity* is a consulting buzzword that, when translated into English, comes down to things that cause megachanges to an industry. Think of regulatory shifts, new technology, natural catastrophes, financial crises, or other extraordinary events that can significantly shift the dynamics of your industry. Any one of these big changes signals a call to action to reevaluate your target market, customer needs, and company offerings.

2. Is there a lack of clear value propositions? In the early days of developing Thomson's transformation strategy, Dick and Tony asked some of the employees of a key division to articulate its value proposition. We couldn't have anticipated the disparate, wide-ranging results. Ask a sample of ten key employees or even ten sales executives to write down your core value proposition, then look to see how much consistency there is.

3. Do you rely more on channel segmentation than customer segmentation? There is no single right way to segment a company's revenue base, but too often companies confuse sales-channel segmentation with end-user segmentation. Segmenting sales by standardized channels such as corporate and government won't uncover similarities and differences in user behavior—informing you about, say, the differences between basic users and those who need to carry out advanced analytics. Consider a segmentation scheme based not on sales relationships but the *user behavior* groups that can inform product development, bundling, and more.

4. Are you facing new customer demands and competition? Changing demand pattern means one thing: you need to dig deeper to understand the customer. Look for shifts in the makeup of total sales and in growth segments, which are often related to new, nontraditional competition or shifts in customer behavior. Ask not if your growth rate is the same, but if the *causes* of growth are the same. You may be growing at the same rate, but how much of that growth now comes from online sources versus traditional

analog sources? Ask not if new competitors have better products, but whether they offer a "good enough" alternative. Finally, ask yourself, if you were in your competitors' shoes, what would you be doing to kill your company?

#6: On Guts

Guts give the thick skin and fortitude to initiate, to ignore whatever criticism you're likely to hear, to stand confidently behind an idea, to persevere, and to know when it's time to take swift action. The most confident, visionary business-builders tell us that their job is to transport others to a vision point they glimpsed months or years earlier—and to close that time gap as quickly as possible.

1. **What terrifies you?** Take your pick: heights, nuclear terrorism, poverty, illness, death. "Only the paranoid survive," Intel cofounder Andy Grove famously wrote, noting that great business-builders and developers *should* constantly worry about competition, product launch dates, cash-burn, and their own ability to attract the best talent, among other things. Acknowledging this kind of paranoia and preparing for it breeds a fortitude that conveys confidence, resilience, and presence of mind. Courage isn't about eradicating fear, but rather about transforming negativity into productivity.

2. **Do you have the Guts to Initiate?** It takes Guts to begin something, both at the earliest stages of business formation and at the later stages when the need for change is evident, but too few people can make that change happen. The Guts to Initiate is the minimum baseline level of Guts that *all* entrepreneurs and business-builders have to have. A credo for business-builders should be above all: *Action, not inaction, and not reaction.*

3. **Do you have the Guts to Endure?** More important than the ability to last—to stick things out—is an individual's strength of mind,

one that recognizes that the short-term sacrifice makes the larger goal worth it. Again, people who boast this strength of mind and persevere through good and tough times are to be admired. The Guts to Endure has less to do with eliminating fear than it does with managing it and gaining perspective on expectations.

4. Do you have the Guts to Evolve? Savvy entrepreneurs know that in order to survive, they must have the self-awareness to adapt to environmental changes and sometimes make drastic modifications. This is the thin line between having the Guts to Endure and the Guts to Evolve. New information, new technologies, new regulations, new competition, and other industry shifts will always be around the corner. One of the most crucial qualities a business-builder can possess is knowing when to stand firm and when to adapt. Successful companies adapt their practices and products to environmental shifts.

#7: To Sell or Not to Sell?

You finally have the chance at an exit. Maybe it came earlier than expected, maybe it came later. Maybe it hasn't come at all but you want to be damn clear on what your perspective on a sale would be. How do you know it is the right time and choice? Many of the serial entrepreneurs in our research had to deal with this "high-class problem" more than once. Here is a question guide to thinking through your options.

1. Do you need to sell? You can avoid this issue entirely by investing cannily in assets with long-term value—and thus extremely long hold periods. Buy things with sound cash flow and "hold-forever" potential. A long-term, value-creating mind-set tends to create fewer exit-timing problems for investors than a short-term, value-capture mind-set. It's really hard to build a company for sale. Build a company for value, and you will have the opportunity for a sale.

2. **Are you trying to value-maximize too much?** The cliché says it best: pigs get fat, but hogs get slaughtered. Don't be the latter. It makes no sense to lunge for every last nickel. When considering a sale, estimate the difference between what you are certain to get now versus some realistic best-case scenario of what you might get later. Factor in the time value of money (a dollar tomorrow is worth a dollar today plus a reasonable rate of return) and compare that with what it would take to get the business to another level in the same time. In other words, consider the risk-adjusted value of staying in the game versus the certainty of taking what you can get today. Will everything continue to work as smoothly? What additional resources might be required, and what execution or market risks are you taking by staying in the game? This is not meant to push you toward a conservative outcome just because an offer is on the table. Instead, it's to get you thinking about what you need to do to create greater value tomorrow relative to the value position you are in today.

3. **Can you take some chips off the table while staying in the game?** As we noted in chapter 4, J. P. Morgan once said, "I made all my money by selling too early."[1] Whether it's through a dividend, a recap, or a sale of part of your stock in a company, if you have a chance to realize some liquidity and if that option makes sense, take a long, serious look.

4. **What is the market context?** If everyone is panting to get into something, it may be time to get out. On the other hand, if the markets are in an economic slump and purchasers are scarce, are you really getting the best price? Ask if this is a buyer's or seller's market.

5. **Do you really want to sell?** Ultimately, it is as much about what you personally want to do as it is about what dollar amount you might realize. Are you happy selling because you will be able to move onto a new venture? Or will you feel as though you have "sold out," especially because you still might love what you are doing and believe you can do more with it? Do you feel that you have fulfilled a large part of your purpose, or is there still much work to

be done? On the flip side, do you think that selling may help you better realize the purpose and potential of your company? Are you confusing your desire to sell with your desire for a different role—for example, do you want to recuse yourself from day-to-day operations while still maintaining ownership? If so, hire someone: management and ownership do not need to be one and the same. Gain clarity by separating financial from nonfinancial reasons.

#8: Are You Humble Enough?

In our experience and research, humility emerges as a defining trait of those who have achieved success. Is a lack of humility preventing you from getting to the next level?

1. Are you willing to embrace your own vulnerability and humility? Vulnerability and humility aren't qualities you would expect to be common among successful business-builders. Yet they are. Risk taking is just a positive euphemism for what we term *active vulnerability*—the willingness to accept the risks and consequences (good or bad) for one's actions. Do you naturally embrace your own vulnerability and humility and accept some degree of failure as a part of any journey?

2. Do you embrace ignorance? If you "don't know what you don't know," it can allow you to have a more open mind and be more fearless in pursuing something new and different. Obviously having knowledge and wisdom is the end goal, but in the beginning of trying something new, *not* knowing isn't necessarily a disadvantage.

3. Are you driven by a deep intellectual curiosity? If you focus continually on improving yourself, you will create more, and "luckier," opportunities. Do you question the norm, have an intellectual thirst for new things, try to sample novel experiences, and seek out

new people? *There is always more to see and more to learn* is a common mantra of the humble and curious.

4. Do people describe you as someone who just works harder? We find that people with humility and intellectual curiosity also tend to be the ones who keep going at it. Some call it drive, others ambition. Whatever you call it and why ever you do it, an unbounded work ethic helps drive success. It is often motivated by a relentless quest to improve. It may even be driven by insecurity. Working harder does not guarantee success, but it does increase the chances of it.

#9: Creating Luck with Optimism and Relationships

The Luck trait is about having the right attitude and the right relationships. Ask yourself these four questions to understand if you are looking at opportunities in a Lucky way, and if you are indeed in the path of the right opportunities.

1. Do you feel lucky (and optimistic)? Extensive research shows that *feeling* lucky can grant confidence, improve performance, and push individuals to aim higher. We can't help but conclude that a questing, questioning perspective allows individuals to recognize and seize chance opportunities. What we often brush away as "luck" is in fact a function of the right attitude and the right relationships, that is, a Lucky Attitude and Lucky Network.

2. Do you focus on the positive before the negative? One of Tony's mentors, the late Jay Chiat, once backed a successful entrepreneur who told us, "The great thing about Jay is that he always sees the good in an idea before the bad." Mavericks and entrepreneurs place the positive before the negative, the optimist before the pessimist. The next time someone pitches you an idea, pause. Now try to focus first on all the reasons this idea might—just might—be a

really, really big idea. Most "out-of-the-box" thinkers and creative entrepreneurs are super-optimists on the outside and critics on the inside. The enduring lesson for us all: lead with optimism.

3. **Do you understand the value of networks?** Don't go chasing and "fan-boying" everyone in a power suit, but mindfully extend the reach, scope, and potentiality of your own personal and professional circles. Luck tends to ripple around the intersection of people, places, timing, and circumstances. By positioning yourself in the way of fortuitous collisions, you heighten the possibility of Luck. In particular, ask yourself if you exhibit the vulnerability, authenticity, generosity, and openness on which Lucky Networks thrive.

4. **Which of the following leadership traits is your weakest link?** Humility, intellectual curiosity, optimism, vulnerability, authenticity, generosity, and openness (see chapter 5 for definitions) are the seven most challenging traits for leaders to master. Which is your weakest link? We know of no one who is perfect across all seven elements, and there is no easy instruction booklet or guarantee that if you possessed all seven that you would become a Zen master of Luck and relationships. But knowing where you are relatively weaker and stronger among these seven business-building leadership attributes will bring more Luck and more rewarding relationships your way.

#10: Reflecting on Failure

In one context or another, you've failed. Use the following five questions to help you recover, learn from your mistake, and improve your approach to the next challenge.

1. **Was this really your True North?** Sometimes people are driven to extrinsic standards of success but they have difficulty finding the

drive to succeed because they do not find meaning in the role or task. Were you driven to succeed by your own True North or by someone else's?

2. Was your own standard reasonable? Failure has much to do with internal expectations. Although it is important to reach for difficult achievements, if things don't go your way, don't let your inner voice berate you any more than you would castigate a hardworking employee. Calibrate your expectations sensibly.

3. Did you try everything possible to succeed? You're the best person to evaluate how much effort you put into your "failed" endeavor. Did you exhaust every conceivable approach in your quest for success? If in evaluating yourself you find that you didn't consider other ways to accomplish your goal, ask yourself why.

4. Are you being macromyopic and overdramatizing the short-term impact of the mistake? Roy Amara, past president of The Institute for the Future, gives his name to a great law of perception. Amara's law states that in looking at events, people tend to overemphasize their short-term consequences and underestimate their long-term impact.[2] So, stop for a reality check on the impact of your mistake. Your action might not be as significant as you thought.

5. What can you learn from your "failure" (including: how do you make damn sure not to repeat this mistake)? Whether your recent "failure" was internally driven, externally driven, or a combination of the two, use it as a learning opportunity. If you could start over, what would you do differently? How would your approach differ? How did your HSGL profile bias you (or not)? Would you simply tweak a few salient details? Be willing to take responsibility. Admit, too, that even in the case of a flawless performance, you might not have succeeded. Again, the key here is to address whatever "failure" you've experienced, explore it, learn from it—and never repeat it.

❾

WISDOM MANIFESTOS

What follows are our Wisdom Manifestos. These are time-tested practices pulled together here as a list of "greatest hits."

The Eight Wisdom Manifestos

1. The Three Golden Rules

2. Be the Best at Something

3. Think Big, Start Small, then Scale Fast

4. Recurring Customers and Revenues Make Life Easier

5. Get the Right Customer

6. Simple Rules and Questions for Getting and Retaining the Best People

7. Accountability Makes or Breaks Your Culture

8. Embrace Failure

Wisdom Manifesto Principle 1: The Three Golden Rules

People > Idea

We cannot emphasize this enough: *people* should always be your top priority. As the founding father of venture capital, Georges Doriot, once put it, "An A-team with a B-plan is always better than an A-plan with a B-team."[1] (See Wisdom Manifesto Principle 6 for tips on building such an A-team.)

Business Model > Plan

Focus on the business model and how you plan to make money instead of on a theoretical financial plan. During the earliest stages of business-building, the *what* of a plan is less important than the *how*. Yes, there are examples of successful entrepreneurs who put off worrying until later about how they would make money. But call us old-fashioned: knowing how you plan to make cash is a good thing. The only reason a business goes out of business is because it runs out of money.

Market Niche > Large Market

Many would-be entrepreneurs spend their time fantasizing about massive markets before they've acquired even a single customer. Even when ideas and concepts burst with gigantic market opportunity, the starting point should always be *which niche, or area, of a big market can you truly dominate?* Remember that a big market brings with it big competitors, so find a niche you can master. Relative market share leadership is the greatest predictor of long-term profitability.

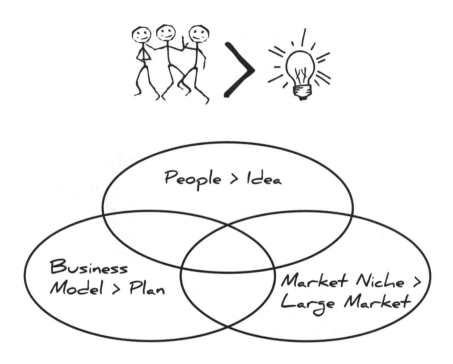

Relative Market Share
always wins

EBITDA
level

RMS

MODEL
$\pi = R - C$

Wisdom Manifesto Principle 2: Be the Best at Something

The best way to align employees and management is to understand the benefit that the business is trying to deliver to its customers. Only four types of consumer benefits matter, and by extension, only four categories of value propositions work.

Best Quality

Richard Branson once commented that being the best at something is a pretty good business model. We couldn't agree more. Consider brands that set a standard, such as Louisville Slugger baseball bats or Stradivarius violins. You don't have to be a sports nut or a classical music aficionado to be familiar with these brand benchmarks. Brands that set unmatched standards are often luxury brands; but even a less luxurious brand like Benjamin Moore can create a long-lasting value proposition by establishing a best-in-class quality reputation.

Best Bang for the Buck

Some consumers will always buy on price; still, best-in-class value doesn't always mean the lowest price, but rather the best quality-to-price ratio. One good example is JetBlue, a company that may not offer the cheapest or best in comfort travel, but that does a superior job of communicating its superior value relative to its price point. Chipotle, Ikea, and Toyota are other illustrations of best-in-class value, and through the years, they've sustained their value propositions.

Luxury and Aspiration

Alongside bang-for-buck players are luxury providers that dangle the experience of a gilded lifestyle to aspirational consumers. Ralph Lauren, Rolex, BMW, and Hermès are among the most masterful purveyors of lifestyle luxury brands. While the luxury segment can take a hit during difficult times, consumers make their way back as the economy rebounds. Not to mention that

many luxury goods consumers have ample discretionary spending, even during tough times.

Must-Have

One of the most attractive value propositions we have seen and studied consists of the *must-haves*. These include basic goods, up to and including certain foodstuffs. At Thomson, we often talked about must-have content, without which business

professionals simply could not do their jobs. One example? The critical legal information and tools Westlaw provides lawyers. As long as there is a case to be filed, lawyers need legal information, and Westlaw is the leading source for that information.[2] There will always be competition between the must-haves, but must-have market leaders ultimately win a great prize: mega value generation.

Reach a New Level!

Does your company's value proposition fit in one or more of the categories above? If not, it's time to adjust. Quit being stuck in the middle. Consider repositioning your offering, and aiming to set a wholly new standard.

3.

Wisdom Manifesto Principle 3:
Think Big, Start Small, then Scale Fast

In execution, it's almost impossible to think big and start big. That's why we always recommend thinking big, starting small, then scaling (or failing) fast. As Professor Bill Sahlman of Harvard Business School has said, "Businesses should begin as a series of sensible experiments."[3]

There's nothing wrong with having a formidable idea, then proceeding to launch miniature versions of it that allow you to continually tweak your concept. Take Chipotle, the Mexican food chain, whose motto and purpose statement are "Food with integrity . . . the very best ingredients raised with respect for the animals, the environment, and the farmers." Steve Ells had a very big idea about food, but rather than executing 100 percent of his vision overnight, he gradually made his way there to really proving concept before sealing it.

Think Big!

Start Small!

Bake Sale:
Anna's Chocolate
Cookies - $5

Scale Fast!

4.

Wisdom Manifesto Principle 4: Recurring Customers and Revenues Make Life Easier

In our previous lives running corporations large and small, we uncovered one business model we love best, one that's based on retaining customers, fundamental cash flow, and the ability to grow that cash flow as the business scales:

Recurring revenue + Fixed cost leverage = Superior cash flow

If you can find a business that has highly repeatable revenues (e.g., high retention of customers year over year) and if you can keep your capital expenditures to, say, less than 10 percent of sales, then you probably have a winner. Businesses that capture this model often correlate with some differentiated form of intellectual property (IP). This can include anything from royalties deriving from content, to franchise fees from branded chains, to subscription revenues from software applications, to licensing fees from technology or patents. Most of these examples require an up-front investment to develop some form of the IP, but if you get it right, you create a defensible moat based on that IP. The excitement VCs have around SaaS (software as a service) and other subscription businesses is driven by the sheer appeal of this "build once, run many times" model, for which the marginal cost of each incremental sale is minuscule.

Another attractive characteristic of this business model is that you often get the cash up front. One example is subscriptions that consumers renew and pay for in advance. Although you can only recognize the revenue in your earnings statement as you deliver the services, you have the benefit of up-front cash.

A cash-up-front business model in which a vast majority of customers renews or returns every year, and where the cost of delivering an additional customer approaches zero at scale—what could be better? Bill Gates himself practices this business model, and it's one that that has worked quite well for him and contemporaries like Marc Benioff at Salesforce.com or Michael Bloomberg at Bloomberg LP.

5.

Wisdom Manifesto Principle 5: Get the Right Customer

There's no such thing as an average customer. Harvard Business School Professor John Deighton offers the example of a hypothetical beverage producer whose research team discovers that 50 percent the world's people love hot tea, while the other 50 percent prefer iced tea. Wouldn't it make sense to manufacture a lukewarm tea that everyone is guaranteed to like? The problem, of course, is that you'd please no one. Steven Levitt and Stephen Dubner, authors of the book *Freakonomics*, offer a more sophomoric example when they point out that the "average" adult in a global sample has exactly one breast and one testicle.[4] In both cases, the mathematical average is an amusing but not altogether useful data point.

Still, companies often make the mistake of developing products and features that appeal to the mean. They pore over aggregate results and averages. What they should be doing instead is disaggregating the drivers of these results and focusing on who, or what, comprises those averages. The key to any successful customer-driven strategy is to understand the dynamic subsegments that make up the average, then develop the right products, prices, and go-to-market plans for each one of those smaller groups.

First, try to understand how you can best and most profitably serve the three top subsegments of your customer base. While seemingly simplistic, this approach often leads to counterintuitive product development or marketing strategies. Example: An analysis of your repeat customer rate may reveal the wisdom of shrinking your current customer base before growing it. Tony once spoke to the CEO of a chain of spas, who shared his goal of convincing at least 70 percent of his customers to repeat a spa service at least once a month. This meant first paying little attention to the vast bulk who were not repeating at this rate. Once he understood what a high-recurring client looked like, he worked hard to get more people like that and less hard to get everyone else.

In this example, the value of a smaller segment of repeat customers is greater than that of many individual customers. Both groups bring in the same levels of short-term revenue, but focusing on repeat customers lowers the cost of sales and marketing over the long term and creates more predictable revenue streams. Quality of revenue is as, or more, important than quantity of revenue.

Online businesses should also apply a discriminating eye to high-level aggregate data analysis. At first glance, high monthly unique counts, or good average usage, may indicate that you have a first-rate product strategy. But by dissecting consumer behavior, you may find that consumers are using only a small percentage of the total functionality you're offering. In this case, focus on the must-have/high-usage features versus the nice-to-have/lower-usage ones. Getting the right product is not too tough if you understand what customers really, *really* want.

Thanks to online tools like Google Analytics or SurveyMonkey, it's easier than ever to capture customer input. But are you interpreting it right? If the survey results indicate widespread variance, it's even more important to pinpoint the subsegment clusters. By using the principles behind well-established marketing analysis (e.g., cluster and conjoint analysis), and grouping results in ranges (e.g., consumers comfortable spending between X and Y versus those in the Y-to-Z range), any entrepreneur can gain a solid pulse of a customer base. He can next consider the pattern differences between these groups and adjust his pricing strategy to consumers' product feature preferences or their willingness to spend.

We're not saying you need perfect subsegmentation. There's no such thing as "perfect"—just as over the years we've learned there's no such thing as "average." Aim to be approximately correct about the top subsegments rather than precisely incorrect about the average.

6.

Wisdom Manifesto Principle 6: Simple Rules and Questions for Getting and Retaining the Best People

Yes, your business idea is brilliant—and infectious—but ultimately it all comes down to people. Accordingly, what's the best way to attract, develop, and retain top people?

When you cast an eye around your social circle, it's a fact that some of your brightest friends hold positions at places that pay little compared with what they could be earning elsewhere. What drives them? Answer: these jobs provide a sense of fulfillment, identity, and purpose that transcend title, position, or salary. By way of illustration, strike up a conversation with an Apple Store or Trader Joe's employee. Now, compare their tenor or tone with that of the employees in 95 percent of other retail establishments. Enough said.

In life, people make love-or-money trade-offs all the time. What can businesses do to minimize this trade-off among employees? They can attempt to create a firmwide balance between intrinsic and extrinsic rewards. Intrinsic rewards, derived from an organization's heart and soul, are an individual's reason and incentive for working at a company. Extrinsic rewards refer to an employee's practical mind and wallet. "The People Rules" lists four points designed toward unlocking the secret of long-term employee loyalty.

Trust us: making employees happy and fulfilled at their jobs is not as hard as it may seem. Part of getting people there is directly correlated with how well you develop and mentor them. We have been extraordinarily lucky to have great mentors. How do you become a great mentor? "Five Secret Questions of Great Mentors" offers a simple framework of the five questions all mentors should be able to ask and understand of their mentees.

The People Rules

Retaining People ⟶ **Intrinsic rewards** > **Extrinsic rewards**

1. **Help her create a meaningful role.** During the interview, ask a prospective employee what she would be doing if she had all the money she needed. Next, explain why her position is critical and how it fits into the bigger picture. We consider this the foundation for long-term retention.

2. **Give feedback.** Do it regularly, honestly, and thoughtfully.

3. **Offer the context of professional development.** Keep your employee's larger career path in mind by asking what she wants to learn most. People like to know where they are heading and that employers care about helping them get there.

4. **Say thank you.** Offer your employee both intrinsic and extrinsic recognition—that is, reaffirm your appreciation for her role or contribution (a simple handwritten note or verbal thanks from time to time goes a long way) and pay her fairly.

Five Secret Questions of Great Mentors

1. What are you trying to accomplish?
2. What are you doing now to help you achieve that?
3. What is slowing you down/stopping you from achieving that goal?
4. What will you do differently tomorrow?
5. How can I help?

Wisdom Manifesto Principle 7: Accountability Makes or Breaks Your Culture

When employees have a vested interest in a company, the company changes. From a collection of far-flung, single-minded parts, it transforms itself into a cohesive organism with a single target: the success of the whole. A company that can create and sustain this high level of accountability will develop a corporate culture predicated on unity, cooperation, and excellence.

So, what's the best way to create accountability in the workplace?

One traditional and default answer is to provide incentives. It is impossible to incentivize unless a company can also measure performance. By nature, incentivizing requires good, reliable information, from the employee to the employer, and vice versa. This is where accountability comes in. Establish a culture of accountability where people know their role and expectations. If those expectations are met, then reward them with incentives. Commonsense stuff, not done as commonly as you would expect.

To ensure firmwide dedication to a unanimously agreed-on goal and cascade that down to every employee, accountability must begin at the top. The CEO and upper management of a company are responsible for setting the tone. The foundation of a great, positive firm culture comes about only when the employees and the company properly align by identifying and sharing identical targets or goals.

Once these are established, the whole becomes greater than the parts. What's more, a positive culture continually strengthens and renews itself.

What underlies your company culture? How can you better align the goals of your company and the goals of your employees? Does accountability begin at the top of your company before it trickles down to employees?

Win with Accountability:

Employees' roles are rarely as clear as sailors' on a boat, but a culture of accountability with aligned incentives drives success in even the darkest storms.

Wisdom Manifesto Principle 8: Embrace Failure

If there is one thing highly accomplished people in their twenties and thirties can do for themselves, it's this: *fail* at least once. Nothing is more damaging to entrepreneurship than a string of advancements based on a Smarts demeanor, or what HR people like to call *high potential*. Once people have absorbed these labels, they become less willing to risk their track record, past successes, and high potential on new or innovative projects.

Of course, failure isn't easy. Often, the residual pain of disappointment, ridicule, and loss never goes away. So why do we encourage at least a one-time brush with disappointment, loss, or blighted expectations? For the reasons we spelled out in the True North question checklist, failure is good when we can reflect on, and learn from, what took place before picking ourselves up and resuming our forward paths. In the best-case scenario, you fail early in your career, and a mentor, a caring colleague, a family member, or a close friend helps uncover a few core truths about you, thus increasing your self-awareness. Make no mistake: failure will happen. What's important is learning how to embrace it and learn from it. Eventually you will be better able to match your capabilities to whatever challenges and future opportunities come your way going forward. Not least, you will also better know when and how to request help at critical moments or similar decision points in the future.

Embracing failure...

...leads to...

...a readiness to take advantage of
other new opportunities!

10

E.A.T.: TAKE THE SELF-ASSESSMENT SURVEY

This chapter provides an abbreviated version of our E.A.T. (Entrepreneurial Aptitude Test) survey, which will give you a directional sense of your HSGL profile. We encourage you to take the more complete survey online at www.HSGL.com. The online test will deliver a more accurate assessment and tabulate your results right away, giving you a snapshot of yourself relative to the entire data set. It will also help us continue to build and improve that data set.

This survey is designed to uncover how you evaluate trade-offs between the attributes that best describe you in the context of business-building. For each pairing, you mark the side that best describes you. It is important to remember that there are no right or wrong answers, so "gaming" your responses toward what you perceive to be the right choices will not benefit you in any way. The test is designed to make you choose between two answers that both seem right to determine whether you lean toward Heart, Smarts, Guts, or Luck.

On your mark, get set, go!

FIGURE 10-1

The E.A.T. (Entrepreneurial Aptitude Test) Survey

For each pair of statements, choose the one that feels the most true to you by filling in the circle. After completing each page, count the shaded circles along each of the four lines on the page, entering each sum in the end boxes.

1. I have been successful thanks to:

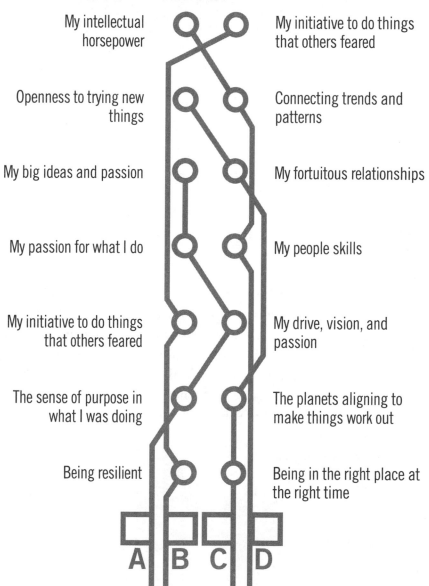

Left	Right
My intellectual horsepower	My initiative to do things that others feared
Openness to trying new things	Connecting trends and patterns
My big ideas and passion	My fortuitous relationships
My passion for what I do	My people skills
My initiative to do things that others feared	My drive, vision, and passion
The sense of purpose in what I was doing	The planets aligning to make things work out
Being resilient	Being in the right place at the right time

A B C D

2. Choose the statement that resonates more:

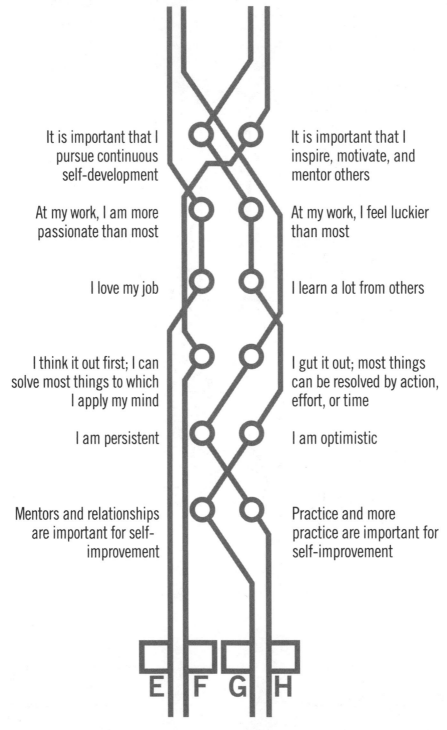

It is important that I pursue continuous self-development

It is important that I inspire, motivate, and mentor others

At my work, I am more passionate than most

At my work, I feel luckier than most

I love my job

I learn a lot from others

I think it out first; I can solve most things to which I apply my mind

I gut it out; most things can be resolved by action, effort, or time

I am persistent

I am optimistic

Mentors and relationships are important for self-improvement

Practice and more practice are important for self-improvement

E F G H

3. My friends would be more likely to say that:

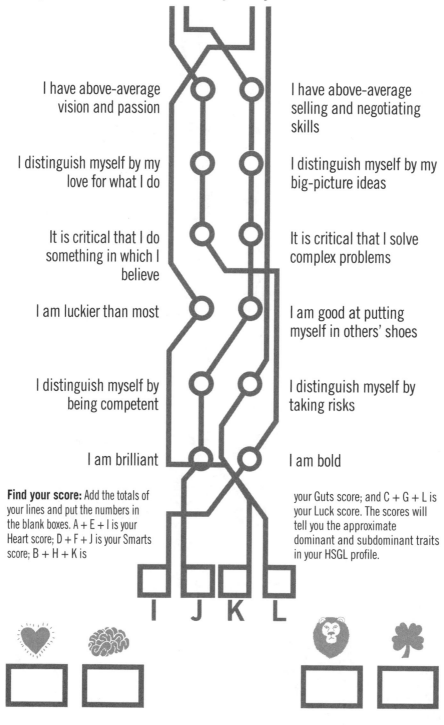

I have above-average vision and passion

I have above-average selling and negotiating skills

I distinguish myself by my love for what I do

I distinguish myself by my big-picture ideas

It is critical that I do something in which I believe

It is critical that I solve complex problems

I am luckier than most

I am good at putting myself in others' shoes

I distinguish myself by being competent

I distinguish myself by taking risks

I am brilliant

I am bold

Find your score: Add the totals of your lines and put the numbers in the blank boxes. A + E + I is your Heart score; D + F + J is your Smarts score; B + H + K is your Guts score; and C + G + L is your Luck score. The scores will tell you the approximate dominant and subdominant traits in your HSGL profile.

I   J   K   L

Interpreting Your Results

How did you come out? What does it mean for you as an entrepreneur or business-builder? Were you surprised with the results? Are you strongest in Heart? Perhaps you have the common profile of a relatively even split between Guts and Smarts, but relatively lower in Heart and Luck? Or are you that Luck-driven person who seems to have just the right disposition and outlook that can take you far? You can flip back to chapter 1 for a quick review of the four traits. Remember that the taxonomy of traits in a given individual is never an either/or situation. In our experience, successful business-builders have all four characteristics in abundance, yet most people *do* tend to lead with either one trait as their dominant characteristic, or with a fusion of any two of the HSGL traits. This simplified book version of the test is more useful for seeing if you are immediately dominant in any one area. The online version at www.HSGL.com displays your percentage distribution of each trait as well as comparisons between your results and the rest of our research database

HSGL is most important as a framing mechanism for self-awareness. The E.A.T. survey, while an important data input to our research and yours, should not be viewed as the sole predictor of who you are. Just as any test or survey—SAT, GMAT, Myers-Briggs, or Predictive Index, to name a few—can serve as informative proxies of scholastic aptitude, working style, or motivational management preferences, they still would not be used on their own to admit students to schools or hire and manage employees. At least, they shouldn't be!

The E.A.T. survey is purposely not labeled the "HSGL Survey" because while it contributes to the HSGL self-awareness picture, it is not the picture in and of itself. Use this diagnostic survey as a lens to approach the material in this book and help guide your own self-reflection about where you are and where you want to be when it comes to business-building potential (especially helpful as you go through the True North questions in chapter 8). As this research is an ongoing work in progress, we'd also love to get your input on how the E.A.T. survey could be expanded or improved and certainly would like your help in passing on the online version to other business-builders.

Wrapping It All Up

There are too many people, courses, and self-help guides that purport to lead you by the hand to the promised land of business success. What we have tried to deliver here are a new framework and some different perspectives that will increase your probability of success, but certainly don't guarantee it. Business-building simply cannot be packaged into an instruction manual.

Remember the statistic that we mentioned near the beginning of the book: two-thirds of the successful entrepreneurs we interviewed did not start with a formal business plan. Instead, they usually conceived their businesses via iterative projects stemming from that place we have called Heart, a trait constituted of purpose and passion, sacrifice and *agape*, and nuance. And there just is no such thing as a step-by-step guide for finding that place.

Nonetheless, the right *principles* can be helpful toward starting, building, and sustaining a business. The foundation is self-awareness. To the extent we have opened your eyes a little, made you stare a little more closely in the mirror, or prompted you to self-reflect with a little more intellectual honesty about your inclinations and skills for business-building, we feel like we have won half the battle. Getting greater self-awareness through the lens and language of our HSGL framework was our primary goal. Our secondary purpose was to communicate the wisdom and habits that we have either developed or seen in action over the years. Have we succeeded? If so, mission accomplished. If not, let us know what to do for the second edition (if we get that chance).

Why do we believe that self-awareness is at the root of business leadership and success? Because without it, you are flying blind. We've focused in this book on using self-awareness to look forward—to understand where you're strongest, where you need to improve, and when you'll need help. But there's also a very important backward use of self-awareness. By looking back at the decisions you've made and how they turned out, you can get better at making decisions.

There's a way to make a habit of this—think of it as one last Smarts habit for the road—that some very smart and successful people have followed through the years. "Whenever you make a key decision or take a key action, write down what you expect will happen," Peter Drucker wrote

FIGURE 11-1

What Type of Business-Builder Are You?

Trait	Defining attributes	You are more of the…	Drivers
HEART 	Purpose and passion, sacrifice (*agape*), and nuance	Idea generator, cultural leader	Purpose, vision, and values driven; "what's the big picture, the big idea?"
SMARTS 	Beyond just IQ; judgment through pattern recognition	Architect, analyst, and strategist	Priorities, people, and performance driven; simplifying ambiguity
GUTS 	Initiation, endurance, and evolution	General and implementer	Progress, execution, and performance driven; "sooner rather than later"
LUCK 	Attitude and relationships	Opportunist, mentor, and mentee	People-centric with humility, curiosity, and optimism

in *Harvard Business Review* in 2005. "Nine or 12 months later, compare the actual results with your expectations."[1] Drucker called this practice *feedback analysis*, and said it was devised by a fourteenth-century German theologian. But lots of people who've probably never heard of feedback analysis do similar things. Warren Buffett writes down the reasons for his investment decisions at the time he makes them so he can look back later to see where he went right or wrong. "Writing down your reasons for making an investment at the time you make it is the only way to learn how to become a better investor," says venture capitalist Vernon Lobo, a former McKinsey colleague of Tony and Tsun-yan's who pointed out this Buffett habit to us. It's a practice we've adopted at our own firm, Cue Ball. That's because otherwise it is too easy *ex post facto* to backward rationalize a decision—which might make you feel better about yourself, but will prevent you from learning anything.

Organizational impact	Strengths	Limitations	Key dilemmas
Purpose, soul, and differentiation	Founding and rejuvenating businesses; providing inspiration and cultural integrity	Emotion overriding logic and judgment; "think big versus start small"	Rich versus king; firing oneself; biggest or best
Strategy and practicality	Conceptualizing and framing situations; priority setting; leveraging knowledge; and scaling businesses	Theory versus reality; left-brain biases; focus on details, but miss the big picture	Compromising to scale; extending growth; becoming "precisely incorrect"
Momentum, tactics, and execution	Taking action at key thresholds of growth—start-up, scale-up, extension, or pivot	Checklist management misses bigger aspiration	Crossing the threshold from enduring to evolving
Opportunity, energy, and openness	Giving and receiving ideas, counsel, and relationships	Overly laissez-faire at times	Embracing failure when bad luck comes

The decisions we make are invariably influenced by our innate biases and predispositions. Heart, Smarts, Guts, and Luck are part of this—by looking back through the HSGL lens, you can better appreciate and learn from why you made the critical business decision you did. Were you primarily Heart-driven at the time? Were you more Guts-oriented and compelled to just act and get things going? Were you more Book Smarts–driven? Or were you overly dependent on the Luck of relationships to help?

There are also, of course, the many cognitive quirks that skew our decisions, as described in the work of Daniel Kahneman, Dan Ariely, and others. And in business and other fields, there are organizational forces at work, too. It can all get pretty muddy. "The essence of ultimate decision remains impenetrable to the observer," John F. Kennedy once said. "Often, indeed, to the decider himself."[2]

This quote inspired Professor Graham Allison of Harvard's Kennedy School (a mentor of Tony's and an investor member of Cue Ball) to write the seminal public policy book *Essence of Decision*.[3] Allison's book uses the Cuban Missile Crisis as a case study to see why and how governments make decisions. Allison puts forth three models—the rational actor (driven by facts, analyses, logic, and utility of payoff), the organizational model (driven by organizational processes and preexisting procedures and plans), and the governmental political model (driven by political constraints). Through each of these three lenses, he illustrates the value of having a framework for greater awareness. Our decisions—and our behavior, our strengths, and our weaknesses—need not remain impenetrable to us. That's what self-awareness is about.

Frameworks illuminate. They illuminate the past, and they illuminate the future. Our framework, of course, is HSGL. It's certainly not the only self-awareness framework for understanding entrepreneurship and business-building, but we have come to appreciate its strengths. We hope you do, too. To close, we offer two things.

First, the HSGL framework one last time, in handy graphic form (see figure 11-1). It's another chance to examine where your strengths and limitations come into play in terms of organizational impact and key decisions.

Second, we'd like to send you off with some encouraging words from one of our interviewees, filmmaker Morgan Spurlock:

I had $200,000 of credit card debt and $50,000 in the bank. I said, I can either take that $50,000 and throw it into this bottomless pit of debt, or, we could make a movie! So we made Super Size Me.[4]

Now *that* is the attitude of a business-builder (one who definitely leans toward Heart and Guts). Others might go about things a bit differently, but the true entrepreneurs and business-builders we met in the course of our research for this book were simply not satisfied with the status quo. They were all out to create some change, some disruption, something new. Take this book as a guide to self-awareness, introspection, and continuous self-improvement along your business-building journey. But, even more important, work relentlessly toward realizing all that of which you are capable. Go out there and do it!

Notes

Chapter 1

1. Christian Silt and Caroline Reid, "Cirque du Soleil Swings to $1bn Revenue as It Mulls Shows at O2," *The Independent*, January 23, 2011; http://www.independent.co.uk/news/business/news/cirque-du-soleil-swings-to-1bn-revenue-as-it-mulls-shows-at-o2-2191850.html.

2. Scott Parazynski, phone interview with author, May 2, 2011. Unless otherwise noted, quotations are from interviews conducted by the authors, 2010 to 2012.

3. Laurel Touby, interview with author, December 2009.

Chapter 2

1. Rupert Merson, *Guide to Managing Growth: Strategies for Turning Success into Even Bigger Success* (London: The Economist/Profile Books Ltd., 2011).

2. Zach Klein, interview with the author, April 20, 2011. Unless otherwise noted, other quotations are from interviews conducted by the authors, 2011 to 2012.

3. The concept here was developed in conversations between Mats Lederhausen and Magnus Kull and mainly inspired by the work of Robert Dilts in *Changing Belief Systems with NLP* (Cupertino, CA: Meta Publications, 1990).

4. "Mr. Narayana Murthy and Infosys: A Case Study of Indian Virtues," *Asia Society*; http://asiasociety.org/business/development/mr-narayana-murthy-and-infosys.

5. David Hornik, interview with the author, February 13, 2010.

6. Sergey Brin, interview with the author, March 2, 2010.

7. Kimbal Musk, interview with the author, February 13, 2010.

8. Authors' analysis of *Forbes* 400 data; http://www.forbes.com/forbes-400/.

9. *The Pixar Story*, directed by Leslie Iwerks (2007; Santa Monica, CA: Leslie Iwerks Productions, 2008), DVD.

10. Kevin Spacey, interview by James Lipton, *Inside the Actors Studio*, Bravo, episode 6.10, aired July 2, 2000.

11. "Mr. Narayana Murthy and Infosys: A Case Study of Indian Virtues."

12. http://www.patagonia.com/us/patagonia.go?assetid=1960.

13. Steve Papa, interview with the author, March, 2011.

Chapter 3

1. Vanna Lee, "What Are You Reading, David Brooks?" *The Book Bench*, *New Yorker*, February 18, 2011; http://www.newyorker.com/online/blogs/books/2011/02/what-are-you-reading-david-brooks-1.html.

2. Jack Hidary, interview with the author, March 3, 2011. Unless otherwise noted, other quotations are from interviews conducted by the authors, 2011 to 2012.

3. John Hamel, interview with the author, January, 2010.

4. Paco Underhill, *Why We Buy: The Science of Shopping* (New York City: Simon & Schuster, 2000).

5. Ben Lerer, interview with the author, February 17, 2011.

6. Eileen C. Shapiro and Howard H. Stevenson, *Make Your Own Luck: 12 Practical Steps to Taking Smarter Risks in Business* (New York: Portfolio, 2005).

7. Steve Schwarzman, interview with the author, March 23, 2011.

8. Keith Ferrazzi, interview with the author, March 2, 2011.

9. Nicholas Piramal, interview with research team, August 2010.

Chapter 4

1. Mike Yavonditte, interview with the author, February 18, 2011. Unless otherwise noted, other quotations are from interviews conducted by the authors, 2011 to 2012.

2. Andrew S. Grove, *Only the Paranoid Survive: How to Exploit the Crisis Points That Challenge Every Company* (New York: Random House, 1996).

3. Dan Pallotta, *Uncharitable: How Restraints on Nonprofits Undermine Their Potential* (Medford, MA: Tufts University Press, 2008).

4. Dan Pallotta, interview with the author, April 25, 2011.

5. Graham Ruddick, "Paul Reichman Gives up Canary Wharf Stake," *The Telegraph*, September 19, 2009; http://www.telegraph.co.uk/finance/newsbysector/constructionand property/6209995/Paul-Reichmann-gives-up-Canary-Wharf-stake.html.

6. Athenahealth, Q3 2011 Earnings Call Transcript, October 21, 2011; http://www .morningstar.com/earnings/earnings-call-transcript.aspx?region=USA&t=ATHN.

7. Based on analysis by the authors on "The *Forbes* 400: The Richest People in America"; Forbes.com/forbes-400.

8. Scott Parazynski, interview with the author, January 2011.

9. J.P. Morgan, quotation as cited in http://blogs.hbr.org/tjan/2009/10/the-art-of-the-exit.html.

Chapter 5

1. Jim Collins, *Good to Great: Why Some Companies Make the Leap . . . And Others Don't* (New York: Harper Collins, 2001).

2. Warren Buffett, lecture at the University of Florida School of Business, October 15, 1998; http://tilsonfunds.com/BuffettUofFloridaspeech.pdf, 23.

3. Kimbal Musk, interview with the author, February 13, 2010. Unless otherwise noted, other quotations are from interviews conducted by the authors, 2010 to 2012.

4. Shunryū Suzuki, *Zen Mind, Beginner's Mind*, ed. Trudy Dixon (Boston: Weatherhill, 2006).

5. Joe Grano, interview with the author, 2010.

6. Tara Parker-Pope, "Phys-Ed: Does Lucky Underwear Improve Athletic Performance?" *New York Times*, July 28, 2010.

7. G. Wayne Miller, *Toy Wars: The Epic Struggle Between G.I. Joe, Barbie, and the Companies That Make Them* (New York: Times Books, 1998), 1.

8. Lysann Damisch, Barbara Stoberock, and Thomas Mussweiler, "Keep Your Fingers Crossed! How Superstition Improves Performance," *Psychological Science* 21, no. 7 (2010), 1014–1020.

9. Christopher Peterson, "The Future of Optimism," *Journal of Personality and Social Psychology* 55, no. 1 (2000), 44–55.

10. Ibid.

11. Richard Wiseman, *The Luck Factor: Changing Your Luck, Changing Your Life, the Four Essential Principles* (New York: Miramax/Hyperion, 2003).

12. Stuart Elliot, "Jay Chiat, Advertising Man on a Mission, Is Dead at 70," *New York Times*, April 24, 2002.

13. Dale Carnegie, *How to Win Friends and Influence People* (New York: Simon & Schuster, 1936).

14. Author interview with Alan Zafran, Woodside, CA, November 14, 2010.

15. Keith Ferrazzi with Tahl Raz, *Never Eat Alone and Other Secrets to Success: One Relationship at a Time* (New York: Currency Doubleday, 2005).

16. Dan Ariely, *Predictably Irrational: The Hidden Forces That Shape Our Decisions* (New York: Harper, 2008).

17. Anthony Tjan, "The Economic Crisis Feeds on 'Macromyopia,'" *Huffington Post*, February 22, 2009; http://www.huffingtonpost.com/anthony-tjan/the-economic-crisis-feeds_b_168985.html.

18. William James, "The Will to Believe: An Address to the Philosophical Clubs of Yale and Brown Universities," *New World*, June 1896.

19. Randy Pausch with Jeffrey Zaslow, *The Last Lecture* (New York: Hyperion, 2008).

20. Phil Pringle, *Top 10 Qualities of a Great Leader* (Tulsa, OK: Harrison House, 2007), 216.

Chapter 6

1. Matthew S. Olson, Derek Van Bever, and Seth Verry, "When Growth Stalls," *Harvard Business Review*, March 2008, 50–61.

2. We thank our purpose-driven partner Mats Lederhausen for this framework.

3. John Hamm, "Why Entrepreneurs Don't Scale," *Harvard Business Review*, December 2002, 110–115.

4. "The Next Big Thing: The Top 50 Venture-Backed Companies," *Wall Street Journal*, March 9, 2010; http://graphicsweb.wsj.com/documents/NEXT_BIG_THING/NEXT_BIG_THING.html.

5. Hamm, "Why Entrepreneurs Don't Scale."

Chapter 7

1. B. F. Skinner, "Superstition in the Pigeon," *Journal of Experimental Psychology* 38 (1948): 168–172.

Chapter 8

1. J. P. Morgan, quotation as cited in http://blogs.hbr.org/tjan/2009/10/the-art-of-the-exit.html.

2. http://www.pcmag.com/encyclopedia_term/0,2542,t=Amaras+law&i=37701,00.asp.

Chapter 9

1. Michael J. C. Martin, *Managing Innovation and Entrepreneurship in Technology-Based Firms* (New York: Wiley, 1994), 311.

2. http://en.wikipedia.org/wiki/Westlaw.

3. Rupert Merson, *Guide to Managing Growth: Strategies for Turning Success into Even Bigger Success* (London: The Economist/Profile Books Ltd., 2011).

4. Steven D. Levitt and Stephen J. Dubner, *Freakonomics: A Rogue Economist Explores the Hidden Side of Everything* (New York: Harper Perennial, 2009).

Wrapping It All Up

1. Peter F. Drucker, "Managing Oneself," *Harvard Business Review*, January 2005, 100–109.

2. Graham Allison and Philip Zelikow, *Essence of Decision: Explaining the Cuban Missile Crisis* (New York: Longman, 1999).

3. Ibid.

4. Morgan Spurlock, interview with the author, March 3, 2011.

NOTES & SKETCHES

Index

Acknowledgments

We want to express our enormous gratitude to all the people who have made this book project and its ongoing research possible. Like many authors who have day jobs, we quickly discovered that book writing takes up time normally reserved for family activities or sleeping. The lack of sleep is OK, but the support of our families throughout this long project deserves our utmost thanks.

Our colleagues at Cue Ball gave generously of their time and talent, and we are deeply grateful to them. Tony Pino, an associate at Cue Ball, did significant research and interviews for this project. Tony also coordinated the work of several interns, designers, and editors throughout the process. As we raced to the finish line on the manuscript, Melanie Wolff, another of our Cue Ball colleagues, read, reread, and reread again each chapter, checking for inconsistencies and gaps and helping to resolve the many she found.

A virtual federation of research assistants helped us with the groundwork of research. Several from the Harvard community and people like Shavi Goel (who interviewed entrepreneurs in India), Maurice Obeid (who interviewed people in the Middle East), and Tsun-yan's colleague at LinHart, Huijin Kong (who researched several business case studies in Asia), contributed in significant ways. Alongside, Amelia Mango and Sarah Schlegel supported research queries. Brian Logan, who joined our team while at Harvard Business School, and Gabe Klein, currently at SK Partners, helped with the compilation and analysis of survey data from our Entrepreneurial Aptitude Test (E.A.T). Speaking of the E.A.T. Survey, we want to give a special shout-out to Conley Zani, whose many years of experience in psychometric testing assessment was essential in helping us with the early development of the survey instrument. Designer Catherine Howell visualized the data with elegant infographics. Alisha Ramos, one of our interns from Harvard College, and Bo Han, who joined us from MIT, were key in the design and launch of the online platform for the project, HSGL.com. We owe them all tremendous thanks for their efforts.

The editorial and production support we had for this book was nothing short of amazing. Peter Smith, a business writer and editor for *O* magazine, has been a wunderkind for helping make the complex clear and for harmonizing our three author voices. From Harvard Business Review Press, we thank our editor extraordinaire, Justin Fox. It's hard to imagine a better editor than Justin, who demonstrated great patience in developing the core ideas of this book and was key in shaping the themes into a consistent and coherent whole. Josh Macht deserves thanks, too, for initially encouraging us to write for *Harvard Business Review* online and eventually to develop this book with the Press. Further, we are grateful to Ania Wieckowski, Allison Peter, and the entire production team at the Press, who maintained the highest levels of quality at every step of the book process.

We also thank the entrepreneurs, leaders, and business-builders who gave so richly of their time in interviews on behalf of this book and our research. The opportunity to spend time with you allowed us to learn not only about you, but about ourselves. Thanks, too, to the hundreds more who completed our E.A.T. Survey and to everyone who supported us in the launch of this book.

Finally, we applaud all the readers of this book who are themselves business-building entrepreneurs, (continually) trying to improve themselves with greater self-awareness and strategic tools. Not only are you the source of big ideas and innovations, you serve as an inspiration for us all to continue pushing to the next level of our potential.

About the Authors

Anthony (Tony) K. Tjan is CEO and Managing Partner of The Cue Ball Group, a venture capital firm based in Boston. Most recently, Tony was Senior Partner with The Parthenon Group, a leading strategic advisory firm, where he remains Vice Chairman. He also served as a long-standing special strategic advisor to the former CEO of The Thomson Corporation, Richard Harrington. In 1996, Tony founded and was CEO of the Internet services firm ZEFER (now an NEC subsidiary), which grew to more than $100 million in annual revenues as a pioneer in commercial Web initiatives. Tony started his career with the global management consulting firm McKinsey & Company, where he focused on consumer and media clients. Tony holds an AB degree from Harvard College, an MBA from Harvard Business School, and was a Fellow at Harvard's Kennedy School of Government. In addition to serving on several boards, he contributes regularly to *Harvard Business Review* and serves on the editorial advisory board of MIT's *Technology Review*.

Richard (Dick) J. Harrington is Chairman and General Partner of Cue Ball, where he helps set overall strategic direction and plays an active role in the sourcing and management of portfolio companies. Before coming to Cue Ball, Dick was President and CEO of The Thomson Corporation, where he led the firm's transformation from a diversified holding company to the world's largest information services and media company, Thomson-Reuters.

Over his eleven years as CEO of Thomson, he quadrupled the cash flow and tripled the market value of the company. Dick has led more than $30 billion in deal transactions, including culminating his Thomson career with the acquisition of Reuters. Dick started his career in a family business and as a CPA with Arthur Young & Co. He serves as a member of the board for Aetna, Xerox, and several Cue Ball portfolio companies. Dick holds a BS degree in accounting from the University of Rhode Island, which presented him with an Honorary Doctorate of Laws in 2002.

Tsun-yan Hsieh is the founder and Lead Counselor of LinHart Group, a leadership services firm that specializes in advising boards and counseling CEOs on issues of succession, leadership trajectory, and top team effectiveness. While his current focus is on Asian companies, he has spent half of his professional career in North America and the balance throughout the rest of the world. Prior to his work at LinHart, Tsun-yan was a Senior Partner at McKinsey & Company.

In a career spanning thirty years with McKinsey, he served clients across dozens of countries and industries, focusing on corporate transformation and leadership development. He founded the McKinsey Center for Asian Leadership, and as Chairman of McKinsey's Professional Development Committee he introduced the firm's apprenticeship model, as well as a leadership model. In 2000, Tsun-yan moved back to his native Singapore to serve as Managing Director of McKinsey's ASEAN practice; he retired in 2008. Tsun-yan currently serves on the boards of Sony Corporation, Manulife Financial, and Singapore International Foundation. He holds a BS degree from the University of Alberta and an MBA from Harvard Business School.

...t the people, idea,
...ind. How can

the idea is sustainable.

academics debate the

...of creating and defending
NICHE. But what
...men anyway? On
...us - what is it that
...create a barrier or edge
...few ideas are unique -
...y not either - so
... a moat and defend
...upon business ideas.

...competitiveness is a relative
...in our consulting and
...focused on a simple
...role for competitive advantage:
...and relationships. Do
UNIQUE or relatively "unique"
...and relationships vis a vis
...respective competition.

...will help illustrate:
...just better pencil. There are som...
...just better and the best tech...
...top people. (As I once lear...from a...
...'s; B'c get C's)
...unique asset ownership (e.g. the Bee's dum...
...an unfair advantage)